"Steve Savino was most instrumental in Century 21® making significant strides in re-energizing the brand's marketing effort. Steve built a world-class marketing team and his efforts culminated with a coveted EFFIE Award for the 'Real Estate for the Real World™' advertising campaign. Steve brought bright strategic thinking and great creative energy to the marketing efforts of the franchise system as we embarked on a change agenda to differentiate the Century 21 brand image in the marketplace."

—Robert Moles, Chairman, **Intero Real Estate Services, Inc.**
(former president & CEO, Cendant Real Estate Franchise Group)

"I taught with Steve Savino on several executive programs for Grand Metropolitan, Plc. (now called Diageo). These programs were called 'Building Brand Equity' (BBE), and they were launched to improve the ability of managers to more profitably manage their brands, accounts, and territories. Steve drew from his experiences to help participants develop frameworks for approaching their own marketing challenges. By combining his real-world experience with an ability to tailor these experiences to participant backgrounds, Steve helped to make BBE a longstanding success within the company."

—Kent Grayson, Ph.D., Associate Professor,
Kellogg School of Management, Northwestern University

"Steve Savino and I worked together at Diageo/Guinness where we partnered with the London Business School to create a major executive workshop on Building Brand-Equity. Steve was the primary driver of the curriculum and instructional design approach. This program was successfully presented to all senior sales and marketing personnel. Steve demonstrated a strong ability to blend academic principles with the real world."

—R. J. (Bob) LaMontagne, Director of Organization Development,
Brown-Forman Corporation

"Steve Savino was the catalyst at Century 21®, making significant strides in re-energizing the brand's marketing effort behind the game of Major League Baseball®. Steve was a leader among our corporate clients and coupled a detailed understanding of his business with a strategic vision, Century 21's relationship with Baseball. Together, Major League Baseball and Century 21 built the Century 21 Home Run Derby® into one of the most prestigious sponsor assets in sports, and Steve was primarily responsible for our success."

—Timothy J. Brosnan, Executive Vice President—Business,
Major League Baseball

"Steve Savino remains one of my 'top' MBA alumni. Additionally, it has been my pleasure to follow his career path and to celebrate his success. Steve and I worked together in a marketing seminar for his subordinates at Century 21®. I can assure you that his people viewed him as a first-class individual and manager."

—James C. Makens, Ph.D., Marketing Professor,
Babcock Graduate School of Management, Wake Forest University

"Savino Global Group has helped our business establish a solid, differentiated position in the luxury fashion service segment; delivered via the internet highway. Steve Savino is an expert at positioning brands for top-line growth. His sound advice and coaching has enabled our marketing team to build a competitive product portfolio, source value-added partners and gain a better ROI from our marketing budget."

—Panagiota Fotoglidou, Chairperson & CEO,
UpperTaste.com, Inc.

The Adventures of *(a real life)* Brand Czar

The Adventures of *(a real life)* Brand Czar

12 Personal-Size Marketing Lessons for Global-Size Results

Steven L. Savino

iUniverse, Inc.

New York Bloomington Shanghai

The Adventures of *(a real life)* Brand Czar
12 Personal-Size Marketing Lessons for Global-Size Results

iUniverse books may be ordered through booksellers or by contacting:

iUniverse
1663 Liberty Drive
Bloomington, IN 47403
www.iuniverse.com
1-800-Authors (1-800-288-4677)

ISBN: 978-0-595-48453-9 (pbk)
ISBN: 978-0-595-60547-7 (ebk)

Printed in the United States of America

Contents

Part 2: New Tools for the Trade—Meaningful Brand Planning   43

Preface and Acknowledgments

MARKETING IS NOT A SPECTATOR SPORT

This book is all about critical success factors. Success factors that represent a snap-shot of those personal adventures and lessons learned in my having led several large marketing teams and related brands to new heights in a highly competitive global environment.

The chapters and pages that follow showcase the key lessons learned and tools of the trade from my years of experience in battling the highly competitive marketing wars on both a global and local market front.

PART 1: LESSONS LEARNED

Part one of this book introduces the marketing rules of engagement that represent confessions about what one must do to succeed in today's highly competitive marketing world. The lessons introduced here are intended to share personal experiences and suggest best practices so that marketers going forward can have the confidence to build on big ideas by slaughtering sacred cows and avoiding the repeat of several prototypical brand marketing mistakes, including but not limited to the misconceptions that re-positioning a mature brand is possible, that consensus will always lead to better decisions, that brand image doesn't really matter or that pricing decisions is just a P&L plug.

PART 2: NEW TOOLS FOR THE TRADE

Part two of this book introduces several new ways to implement the traditional tools for the trade including a new strategy model called the *Brand Activation Matrix*, designed to complement the Boston Consulting Group's Growth-Share

Matrix Model; a new approach to utilizing SWOT analysis whereby a manageable number of *Must-Win-Battles* are crafted and leveraged throughout the organization; a brand positioning model that truly differentiates and leads to a brand promise that acts as the brand's central business proposition from which all initiatives that require funding are measured against; a new product development growth strategy model that is based on identifying industry segment 'Hot Spots' that act as the foundation for ideation development and the new products funnel for customer target setting, R&D, beta testing and national/international launch; and a brand marketing annual planning template that leverages the brand's key issues and challenges for strategies, action plans and budget development, ROI and measurement criteria.

These tools were not conceived and written by a marketing academic, but by a real-world marketing practitioner.

EXPERIENCE MATTERS

The insights presented throughout this book are grounded in experience—not theory, and they have universal application no matter what industry or product/service category one competes in.

The crafting of winning brand strategies is the cornerstone to any marketer's professional success and personal growth. My hope is that this work acts as an enabler for one to rise to new heights in strategy development, action plan prioritization and leadership through bold courage in accepting responsibility for planning and directing the total marketing effort of a company's brand.

ACKNOWLEDGMENTS

Several people and many companies and brands were influential in my writing this book. Let me offer my personal thanks here first to Ruth Fein Wallens for your great enthusiasm in this project and for tremendously helping me with interviews for the storylines and concepts, editing the work and providing suggestions on tonality, writing style and case study examples. Also, personal thanks go to Larry Bouts and Robert Moles for teaching me so much about leadership; professor James C. Makens of Wake Forest University and the late professor Adolph S. Butkys of Villanova University for teaching me so much about strategic marketing; Lee Garfinkel for teaching me so much about advertising; Kevin Meany, Ted Winters and Alyse Kobin for teaching so much about promotions, PR and special events marketing; Bruce McDonnell for teaching me about the strategic impact of new product development; Barbara Martino for teaching me how best to work with agency support teams; Roland Grybauskas and Jiotta Fotoglidou for teaching me so much about the internet and interactive marketing strategy; and to all of my marketing colleagues, especially all the former V.P.'s, directors, managers and others that worked for me and put-up with me across several organizations and not only inspired me to be the best I could be but challenged my thinking, thus always making for a better product in the end.

Special thanks go to the following great company organizations and their related brands where I was able to conceive and execute my best brand marketing work over a 25 year period of time: General Instrument Corporation (now part of Motorola), The Anheuser-Busch Companies, Inc., The Southland Corporation, Diageo (formerly Heublein, Inc., a division of GuinessUDV North America), Time Warner, Inc., Century 21® Real Estate Corporation, Unilever N.V., PLC/ UBF North America and Cynergy Data Corporation.

Also, very special thanks go to the legendary Ringo Starr for making me feel as if I was the fifth Beatle and treating me just like I were a member of his All-Starr Band, and to *Major League Baseball*® and, in particular, hall of famer Cal Ripken Jr. for teaching me about dignity and humility and for that coveted autograph ball he signed to my daughter, with the very special inscription that he wrote, *"Patrece, discover baseball. Ask Dad."*

Finally, I would like to thank those closest to me for their love, patience and support, especially my daughter Patrece who is the breath of fresh air in my life and my one pride and joy. It's every father's dream to have a child he can call his best friend.

Steven L. Savino
CEO & Brand Czar
Savino Global Group, LLC.

PART 1

Lessons Learned from an
Estranged Marketing Chief

Chapter 1

Lesson One — Image Really Does Matter

"Creativity is the ability to see relationships when none exist."

—Thomas Dish

A true marketing czar might be measured by the walls within which he lives. Not by the colors or furnishings, or how high the ceilings rise. No. We're talking important stuff. Like what hangs on the home office walls; what prominently displayed celebrity autographs hang next to the bathroom sink. We're talking memorabilia—the coveted "stuff" we accumulate along the life of our careers that tell the stories of our accomplishments—our promotional successes, the proud moments and measures of our otherwise private public lives. After all, no one knows who's behind that great TV ad you just called your wife or husband or significant other into the room to see. But chances are, some marketing exec has that TV commercial Star's autographed photo or t-shirt hanging somewhere on the wall behind a glass case.

While not prominently displayed, I certainly have my share of marketing war treasures. As it should be, the two closest to my heart reflectively bridge business and pleasure … career and family.

I grew up listening to the *Beatles*®—never wore John Lennon style spectacles, but admittedly there were a few Nehru shirt collars and at least one Nehru jacket hanging in the closet. So when I say I have a personally signed Ringo Starr drumhead in my treasure box, you might understand the heart-skip WOW factor that can still come when taking a quick glance.

3

When *Century 21®*, the largest residential real estate company in the world, wanted to make up for a lack of differentiation among competitors, and strategically address the growing consumer trend toward internet-based self-navigation of the home-finding process, I was brought in to rebuild the brand's equity (yes, the drumhead connection is coming). And oh what a grand time it was for me and my marketing team. We built high profile strategic partnerships with Major League Baseball® (MLB), as well as with legendary Beatle and world-wide icon Ringo Starr—together capturing a *PROMO Magazine* Best Promoted Brands Award for 2001, not to mention a *BrandWeek* Cover Story in March 2000. Promotional event sponsorships like the Century 21 MLB Home Run Derby®, and the national tour of Ringo Starr and his All-Starr Band, brought enormous opportunities for brand publicity and thereby enhanced the brand's overall media impressions (more effectively and efficiently than what traditional media buys could have done alone). Simultaneously, a new advertising campaign led to several highly visible advertising commercial executions, including one that includes Ringo. That campaign, *"Real Estate for the Real World™"* was deemed a measurable success story capturing a coveted EFFIE Award for advertising effectiveness. Not bad for what once was thought of as a sleepy real estate brand in a not so exciting—in fact—boring industry.

Sales and Brand Equity results:

Century 21 average home sale prices out-paced the industry by rising by more than 7% overall (the overall industry average was around 5% growth).

Sales leads, secured via promotional sweepstakes entry forms tied to the association with MLB and the Home Run Derby, were well over 500,000 per year (characterized as "real leads" by sales agents nationwide).

Local incremental Media Impressions:

+300 million from MLB

+180 million from Ringo

But why was this branding effort so successful? Was it simply about high exposure and recognizable associations? No. Its success illustrates the power of crafting a *single-minded brand positioning*.

Historically, real estate companies stuck mostly to what was considered to be institutional advertising, designed primarily for name recognition, with little attention to creating real differentiation or to building a brand identity and image that sets that brand apart from the competition. Case in point, Century 21 did not reap market share benefits from consumer knowledge that it is the largest residential real estate company in the world. In fact, before executing our strategy, the Century 21 brand's average home sale price trailed the industry average by about 20 percent. Frankly, there was a "so what" factor at play. Being bigger didn't mean they were different or better in any way, shape or form. In fact, Century 21 *"suffered from sameness"* when compared to other competing nationally branded real estate companies—i.e. *RE/MAX®, Coldwell Banker®,* etc. What was needed was a break-out creative strategy, one that created a far more differentiating identity, a stronger branding of the company and its services. And, to be successful, this single-minded brand identity needed to be driven by advertising and promotional campaigns that stood out and captured the hearts and minds of consumers, franchisees and local sales associates.

Positioning is everything in marketing. Once you get this right—a single-minded brand identity—everything else falls into place almost as if on auto pilot.

Case Study: *Century 21® Real Estate Corporation*

Critical Insight: The new *Century 21®* communications platform needed to deliver against a strategy centered on making the brand more approachable. Why? Consider this fact—consumers associate the home-buying process with tremendous anxiety. Making the brand more approachable by making the brand more fun, particularly through the use of self-deprecating humor, reduces that consumer anxiety and thus apprehension about the process of buying or selling a home. This strategic approach had real legs—real potential to be break-through.

Campaign: *"Real Estate for the Real World™"*
Campaign Tone: use of self-deprecating humor that brings real fun to the brand.

One series of television ads pictures home buyers with a real estate agent offering unimaginable services, i.e., arranging for utilities, cable TV and home entertainment. The buyers are offered a choice of piped-in music through a new built-in entertainment system or (camera pans to Ringo Starr and his All-Starr Band in the living room) as the sales agent/announcer adds: *"cable-TV, entertainment or Ringo Starr?"* This cues Ringo's classic Beatles song-like response: *"with a little help from my friends,"* as he points to the All-Starr Band standing behind him.

In another ad, a couple is discussing mortgage terms with a banker. The loan manager offers the home buyers a zero interest loan, no monthly payments for a year, and states, *"oh, by the way, I threw in some extra cash just in case you need it."*

In yet another TV spot, the buyer notices a brand new in-ground swimming pool has been installed, and states, *"they put in a pool before they left?"* From which the sales agent explains *"we can take it out if you'd like."* Naturally, the home buyer's response was a resounding *"NO."*

Then the consistent payoff at the end of every ad …
"If buying a home were this easy," according to the campaign tag line, *"you wouldn't need Century 21. Real Estate for the Real World."*

REWIND

How does the largest residential real estate company in the world decide to completely change the way the industry markets, and the way its own corporate culture thinks about customers and service, to drive a new strategy?

In this case, it started from the top. The CEO knew change was needed to differentiate the Century 21 brand, positioning it as a leader, where image-wise it once was and where it belonged. What he didn't know was how fundamental a change was necessary, what it would look like, or what it would take to get there. What he did know was that he didn't know. And this is the key to hiring an experienced brand marketer, a "brand czar" so to speak, and empowering that person to get the job done.

The first question a new person coming in to lead the marketing charge needs to be able to answer, on any brand, is simply this: *what place in the customer's mind do we want to own?* In other words, what is the *Core Value* of the Brand? What is the *Brand Essence* that leads us to a *Brand Promise* that is differentiating and acts as the brand's business blueprint or business proposition? The brand positioning pyramid model (introduced in chapter 8) remains one of several very effective tools for helping to quickly organize the critical success factors that answer this fundamental question. Often, new market research is designed, carried out and analyzed to support this process. But other times, as was the case with Century 21, we are led by past experiences, intuition and yes, gut instinct.

C-level execs come in all shapes and sizes, and in all degrees of need for hard data to back up a plan recommendation. Here, it was clear that the need to move fast was more important than the need for precise research to back-up every argument or recommendation. Calculated risks had to be taken in the interest of speed and budget constraints. So, the new marketing strategy, centered on a single-minded, own-able and defendable brand positioning, was crafted from a combination of existing consumer research, industry management expertise and my personal experience having been a consumer home-owner and home-seller. I was hired June 22, 1998 (I remember this date only because it's my birthday). By January 1, 1999, we were ready to launch a complete, fully integrated new brand marketing strategy, ready to air the new advertising campaign, and ready to implement new, value-added promotions, public relations initiatives, new products/services, and new internet-based strategic initiatives.

Here's what we had to work with …

Beliefs and Supporting Facts:
- Buying a home is typically the largest single investment a person will make in his/her lifetime.
- The home-buying or selling experience is riddled with apprehension, driven by anxiety.
- Buyers are asked to bet on the ego of the agent *("I'm a million dollar seller")* instead of a strategy to market your home to sell faster, and for a higher price, than the three for sale your home competes against down the street.
- Consumer awareness and market share was high for the Century 21 brand, compared relative to its competition. Brand Equity was low relative to several key competitors; especially the premium-imaged ones that were considered to be more local or regional companies (i.e. *Sotheby's®, Long & Foster®, Weichert®,* etc.).

The unique thing about a franchise system, like Century 21, is that each franchisee pays into a marketing trust fund. And the fund, by contract, has to be spent. Period. Yes, a $45–$50 million budget is nice to have. But one should never take budget into account when developing strategy. Let me repeat this. One should never take budget into account when developing strategy. If Century 21 had a $1 million budget, I would have developed the same strategy. How I executed it would obviously have been different. It now bears repeating that $45–$50 million is a nice marketing budget to have and to hold … and to spend.

Moving forward, I was already convinced of the answer (and could approach our corporate executive leadership team with the courage of my convictions) that the right single-minded brand positioning strategy for Century 21 was all about first acknowledging, then alleviating *Anxiety* and thus, *Apprehension*. Alleviate a person's anxiety and their apprehension falls by the wayside. What was needed now was the buy-in from franchisees—50 percent of whom could be expected to love the new strategy, 50 percent would likely hate it. The goal was to make sure that the 50 percent who loved it were the right 50 percent—the one's who really drove the business. Why is this important? Because in the world of franchising, word of mouth travels fast and furious, and there are leaders and followers, along with the usual wannabes, who can be intentionally negative opinion leaders. Convince the thought leaders and the followers will fall in line.

How did we do this? First, we pulled together a dozen representative franchisees for a series of marketing development work sessions. The president and CEO welcomed them, introduced me, and told them they were personally selected because this was important; the company valued their opinion; that the sessions would directly translate into an exciting new marketing direction and strategic plan of attack. And, most importantly, the CEO was there to tell them personally that he had confidence in me and had already bought into the need for change. He was counting on them to cooperate, and with the help of his new "marketing czar," to contribute to the development of the strategy. After all, where was it written that a real estate brand had to *"suffer from sameness?"*

As planned, I spent the first two sessions teaching real estate franchisees about brand marketing. I walked them through basic branding strategy. I taught them how to utilize a brand positioning pyramid model to instill discipline and focus in the development process. We reviewed a number of case studies on other brands, outside the real estate industry, and completed exercises that illustrated the critical importance of crafting a single-minded, own-able and defendable brand positioning (the place in the customer's mind we want to own).

Numerous, interesting case studies exist on brand positioning, including the quick review examples below that C21 franchisees and I dissected together:

Volvo® = *safety*	Volvo ≠ style & performance
Smirnoff® = *mixability*	Smirnoff ≠ fashion
Dove® = *moisturizers*	Dove ≠ purity
Six Flags® = *thrill*	Six Flags ≠ family fun
Ivory® = *purity*	Ivory ≠ deodorant soap
Head & Shoulders® = *fights dandruff*	Head & Shoulders ≠ smooth & silky

Now, by the third planning session, I led the franchisees through the process of creating the brand positioning for Century 21 using the positioning pyramid model (see chapter 8). We talked about the consumer experience—the psychology that surrounds buying and selling a home. We acknowledged that Century 21 is very available and recognizable. In the end, this team of realtors came up with a *Core Value* for the brand that they took complete ownership of—not only because it was right, but because they believed they had created it themselves. Exhibit 8-10 in chapter eight illustrates this positioning development strategy for Century 21. It was from this work that Century 21 was now ready and able to launch a new marketing strategy driven from the core essence of a single-minded brand promise dubbed *"the anxiety antidote."*

The representative franchisees went home happy and excited about what might come out of their efforts. I could now translate this new brand promise into a business proposition, develop a creative brief or blueprint, and a comprehensive marketing communications plan. And the best part, I could open the annual convention of 12,000+ Century 21 franchisees and sales associates saying that their realtor counterparts played an integral role in the development of the advertising and promotional campaign they were about to see.

The lights went down in the convention hall in Las Vegas. The new TV commercials went up. The standing ovation was blissful. I felt like a Rock Star … oh what an injection of confidence!

The two marketing war treasures closest to my heart? Coincidentally, they're both from my association with Century 21.

Ringo Starr, who when pressed to autograph anything, simply swirls the pen into a vaguely recognizable $\mathcal{R}$ _____, signed a drumhead for me that says: *"To Steve, WOW!"* signed Ringo. This was special. This was personal.

Now, just when I thought it couldn't get any better, the legendary baseball hall of famer, Cal Ripken Jr., after working together on advertising and promotions for the Century 21 Home Run Derby, asked me about my then 4-year old daughter. Suddenly, and with out prompting, he signed a baseball for her with the words, *"To Patrece, discover baseball. Ask Dad"* signed Cal Ripken Jr. It was like magic for a baseball fan of 30-something years.

Chapter 2

Lesson Two — Consensus is the Negation of Leadership

"Search the parks in all your cities and you'll find no statues of committees."

—David Ogilvy

It can't be said more simply. Try to please everyone and you please no one. In marketing, the clear stars are those who are prepared to put their careers on the line—to stand up for something they strongly believe in—even if it means going against the biases of significant others in the organization; not to mention the sacred cows that have lingered over head for years. The pay off is when you get the grand slam you envisioned, that others just couldn't see.

No doubt committees have their place—they can converse, contemplate, and even criticize. But they can not create! Yes, a successful marketing exec should gather input from several key people and related sources. And if the best way to do that happens to be in a committee, then go ahead and make it happen. Obviously bringing people together to garner ideas and feedback is all good. It makes people happy. It helps them "buy in" to a concept or strategy. But nothing is worse for creativity than marketing by committee (except maybe creating advertising designed to simply please market research).

Marketing by consensus virtually always stifles the creative process—if not by slowing down momentum or rejecting promising ideas, then by the ultimate watering down of a strong, cutting edge or out-of-the-box concept or campaign. This is where leadership must prevail. An organization with strong marketing

11

leadership is able to thank people for their input—even take it into consideration. Then, the marketing decision maker makes the final call.

When *Six Flags® Amusement Parks* decided to revamp its marketing strategy, I was faced with several obstacles—a decentralized management team: 12 individual parks, 12 individual ways of thinking, 12 vice president's of marketing with several different advertising agencies, and numerous, different advertising campaigns. Yet all of the parks were virtually the same! I didn't need to put on my thinking cap to figure out the major challenges ahead. This is the stuff of marketing czar nightmares—the never stopping carousel with too many ups and downs, brightly painted players alternately vying for attention, and no way to turn around or get off—just another round-about in the same direction. The only way to move forward would be to pull the plug, start from scratch and slaughter the sacred cows.

Ironically, there clearly was consensus—the wrong consensus. Park managers did not want to give up their control. They believed the answer to higher profits was more body turns through the park entrance turnstile. They admittedly would never turn away the Teens who come to ride their 90 mph roller coasters, but they believed in the need to market to young families to increase the number of attendees coming through the turnstiles of their parks. Yet, the parks offered virtually nothing for this pre-teen audience. They were too young to ride the coasters and there was very little in the way of kid rides for really, really young kids to gravitate to.

Management's way of thinking needed to change. Ronald Reagan once said, *"Facts are stubborn things."* And in this case, the facts were undeniable.

This is *'this'* and that is *'that.'* *'This'* is Not *'That'* and *'That'* is Not *'This.'* Six Flags is a thrill park that is all about high-speed roller coasters and active participation. Six Flags is Not Disney®, nor is it Disney-like. It is not a vacation destination for high-quality, passive entertainment. Instead, Six Flags is a local destination for high-quality participative entertainment.

A positioning strategy is only effective when it is single-minded, own-able and defendable. The right strategy for Six Flags was centered on a positioning with *THRILL* as the cornerstone—its *Brand Essence*. Review exhibits 8-5, 8-6 and 8-7 in chapter eight for a complete review of the Six Flags brand positioning development. And once again, when the positioning strategy is right, from the start and from the top, the balance of the marketing plan simply falls into place. Here, the key word was TOP.

CASE STUDY: *SIX FLAGS® AMUSEMENT PARKS*

Critical Insight: The success of a new marketing strategy for *Six Flags®* was completely dependent on the ability of a new-hire chief marketing and sales exec to walk in the door and change the core culture of the organization. Asking park managers to straighten the twisted loops and curves of their wildest coaster rides might have been easier.

Marketing Strategy: The parks needed a single corporate identity, and a single-minded, exciting new marketing and advertising campaign. Six Flags Theme Parks were all about *THRILL.*

Tool: intimidation … with a compassionate tone.

REWIND

It was critical that park managers felt an absolute degree of intimidation about some marketing czar coming in and changing their world. Why? Because it would make them listen. Without the intimidation factor, without recognition that this particular person knows more than they do about this particular subject, it would be too easy for them to be dismissive. The challenge was to get them to feel this. After all, weren't they the experts about their business? Didn't they know what was best for their parks? Operationally, for their parks? Maybe. Emotionally, for their consumers? NOT.

The key element was leadership. Here, the new CEO of this parent company was from outside the theme-park industry; he was not married to the traditional amusement park mentality. He was able to evaluate my track record and place it in the context of what he wanted to accomplish. The players were different. The situation was different. But what needed to be done was not all that different from what I had successfully done many times in the past—differentiate a brand and position it for growth.

We sat together and I boiled it down. *"Here are the key issues and challenges, beginning with the fact that the parks were price discounting way, WAY too much given that the primary target audience consisted of relatively price insensitive teenagers."*

Here, the profit upside was great—reduce the dependence on discounts and raise top-line revenues by as much as $300 million when it's all said and done. I went on, *"Here are the strategic pieces I'll put in place to address these issues and challenges. You buy-in and hire me, or you don't."* It was a clear case of presenting my self with the courage of my convictions. I concluded, *"This is the way I'll do it. This is what needs to happen to be successful. And your support must be visibly secured."*

I insisted that Larry (CEO) introduce me at the first meeting of all of my direct reports. Seated around the corporate conference room were the park-level marketing vice presidents, directors of group sales and sponsorship, and promotions and creative services directors. Larry was to introduce me, then leave. I had to set the tone when it came to marketing and sales. The people in this room would have to look to me first, not to him, from this point forward.

"I want to address your questions and concerns," I began. *"But first I want to be clear about what we as a group want to value going forward ... And on these principles there will be no compromise."*

Now, when they later heard that there won't be 12 different marketing campaigns and multiple advertising agencies, (or in other words they are losing control of marketing their own parks) the group could come back to a clear answer as to why this must happen. *"Because this is what we value."*

The short list started with a single-minded brand strategy and ended with measurable targets. So, what were these members of the current management team feeling as they gazed seemingly dazed at each other around the table? If I was successful so far, the little voice in each of their heads would be whispering: *"WOW, he's confident."* And it would be clear as a sunny park day that I already had the necessary buy-in from the top to move forward—with them (hopefully) or without them (if need be).

The New Uncompromising Values ...

1 brand across 12 parks

1 clear strategy directed from corporate, executed at the park level

1 single agenda with a marketing and sales organization designed around the strategy, rather than visa versa

All Targets will be measurable

Marketing effectiveness and efficiencies will improve

"How we accomplish these things is what we're going to build on over the next several weeks," I continued. This, so they would feel the sense of urgency we needed to move forward. Then, back to intimidation. *"Some of you will struggle with letting go of the past,"* they were told. *"But this won't slow us down one bit or get in the way of progress."* In other words, there's a new high-speed freight train moving out and I suggest you hop on.

One thing was clear walking into this initial meeting. This was one of those times to put an agenda of being effective ahead of an agenda to be liked. There would be time for the usual introductions of each manager and some personal notes about myself. But I believe that most people want a challenge—most want to be part of something great and successful. By going into this meeting fearless—showing the current management team a tone with no ambiguity, only the strength to see through what I believe—it opened the door to change that would make room for them to jump on their own river of rapids raft, rather than leave them behind watching everyone else enjoy the ride.

All of this said, intimidation factor in place, it was time to humanize myself and the process that lay ahead. My deliberate brand czar tone was likely to have them experiencing a degree of shock. And we didn't want shock to lead to fear. Fear leads to *"I'll do what you ask without thinking,"* without challenging, rather than *"I'm challenged with working with you to make things better."* The reality is that I want to be seen as approachable; I want people around me who are comfortable enough to ask questions and tell me what they think. But in the end, leadership through consistency and follow-through must rule.

So as the meeting continued, *"I'm Steve. I have a daughter who's the most precious thing in my life ... I'm a big Yankees fan, so all of you Mets fans need to leave now ... (smiling)."*

Chapter 3

Lesson Three — Never Let the Accounting Dictate the Strategy

"And the trouble is, if you don't risk anything, you risk even more."

—Erica Jong

Now and then, I'm fortunate enough to meet one of my best old friends at Madison Square Garden in New York City for the Big East® Conference Basketball Tournament, then to dinner at La Mela, a favorite restaurant in the Little Italy section of lower Manhattan. While Dick and I stare at the menu as if we don't already know what we'll have, I find myself smirking about something he said to me a few years ago over a spicy plate of calamari.

Dick, now retired, at the time was VP of Finance at the old Heublein Company when I was brought in as VP of Marketing. Years later, with a crusty end of garlic bread in his hand, he says, *"Ya know Steve; I didn't like you when I first met you."* We both worked on the company's flagship brand, *Smirnoff® Vodka* (known as the company's crown jewel brand).

"Why is that," I leaped in.

"Because you were a marketing guy, so I knew you'd be a headache." Without asking for more detail, he continued. *"Marketers are irresponsible. It's a good thing us finance people are around. Marketers spend money like drunken sailors. But at least sailors—they spend their own money."* And this coming from one of my best buddies. Ouch!

Dick couldn't help it. It's in his DNA. Finance guys think marketing is all about spend and waste. They view all budgets, including marketing, as costs. Marketers know that marketing dollars are an investment. I believe marketing can make more money for an organization, by investing money in the brand, than finance departments can by cutting budgets.

Still, as we walked through the city streets, Dick would point at the homeless people we'd see, with only their cardboard boxes to protect them from the elements. *"This is where all past marketing chiefs wind up,"* he'd say. *"See what you have to look forward to,"* he'd go on. To this day, every time I see a poor homeless guy on the street, I think of Dick … and apparently my future retirement.

I hate to think about all of the great ideas that get passed on by an organization because they fly in the face of what the finance and/or accounting departments' value. Case in point, look at gross margin versus gross profit dollars for a perfect illustration. A company introduces a new product or initiative. Accounting—an administrative function—will measure its success (or potential success) by gross margin, a percentage measurement. Marketing is strategic rather than administrative. We know you can't take percentages to the bank. Gross profit dollars, on the other hand, make an attractive bank deposit. Incremental gross profit when combined with market share measures, are how any new initiative should be benchmarked.

Remember this fact; accountants don't drive the revenue line. They just count it. It's marketing and sales that must be bold and combine forces to take risks to generate revenues. For strategies to work, marketing must take the lead, and create a workable, realistic plan. Sales then must execute in-market, by customer, against that plan. Technically, it is the job of finance/accounting to simply calibrate and report results out to the organization. After all, isn't this why they're called bean counters?

All too often a marketing department is discouraged from launching a great idea or product most effectively because the gross margin just isn't good enough for the bean counters to buy in. This is where we can learn the most from examples of lost opportunities. A critical element of the introduction of a proposed new concept or product must be planning for and presenting realistic goals. But even more importantly, to beat down the numbers dogs, a successful marketing exec will put everything on the line to get others in the company to look at the bigger picture. And sometimes, still, it just doesn't work.

CASE STUDY: *RAGU® PASTA SAUCE*, a Unilever brand

Critical Insight: The *Ragu®* brand had experienced significant brand equity erosion, which led to heavier and heavier levels of price promotion in order to hold volume levels. A new marketing strategy would reinforce the brand's ingenuity—by creating customer associations of Ragu with additional uses other then just as a sauce for pasta occasions.

Tool: A new higher-end product, *Ragu® Rich & Meaty®*, is conceptualized and launched as a first step to broadening the use of Ragu sauces beyond pasta—designed specifically to increase the use and re-trial of an old, highly recognized, yet tired, and declining brand.

REWIND

What ultimately happened to Ragu Rich & Meaty isn't as relevant as what we can learn from the challenges faced and choices made along the product development and marketing road. From the beginning, the company party line (CEO, CFO) was clear: don't introduce anything in the Ragu brand portfolio that has less than a 50 percent gross margin. The problem with this is that when you arbitrarily throw out a margin number, it has nothing at all to do with the marketplace, and sometimes nothing to do with the ultimate goal of the product launch. This is where you need to stop. Before introducing any new concept, and certainly before a new product launch, you need to decide: *"Can I successfully (and am I willing to) compromise the quality, size, distribution and/or packaging that I believe will make this a successful consumer product in order to meet the organization's dictated gross margin number?"* And, equally important, is the company willing to make the right compromises?

The margin problems with Ragu Rich & Meaty were simple enough. The original product offering included a full half-pound of quality ground beef and was introduced to the market in a 16 oz. jar. So while there were all kinds of value added to the base brand's original 12oz. pasta sauce jar, often priced at $1.99 or lower, there was a new, critical unknown. Is that same consumer willing to pay $3.79 or higher for a Ragu product? This was the price floor necessary to even come within striking distance of achieving the dictated 50 percent gross margin target mark. In fact, at $3.79 retail, without altering the product's ingredient composition (quality risk?) and/or packaging (size?), we would fall short of reducing costs to the level that was needed to achieve the gross margin goal. So back to the question at hand—If the answer to the question whether consumers are willing to pay $3.79 or higher for a Ragu product is NO; then product compromises are necessary.

It was recommended that the new Ragu Rich & Meaty be introduced in a smaller, trial-size jar for a lower, more familiar introductory price. The other option was to reduce the quantity of meat in the 16 oz. jar. But with this move, you're compromising on the quality and added value that is the sole reason for a consumer to pay more for this Ragu product. And with less meat, it becomes difficult to market the sauce for alternative uses or usage occasions, i.e., Sloppy Joes, chili or meat dip for chips, meat sauce over hot dogs or for chicken sandwiches, just to name a few.

Strategically, the margin game was getting in the way of concept and ingenuity.

Market research told us people wanted meat in their pasta sauce, but the introduction of a significant quantity of quality meat gave us much more opportunity to market the product for additional uses. The new Ragu Rich & Meaty enabled us to physically merchandise this Ragu brand in places other than the pasta aisle. Now we could promote the product around several, higher traffic perimeters of the store, including in the bread section for Sloppy Joes, in the snack aisle as a meat dip, in the meat aisle with chicken, with chili sauces and beans, etc. The in-store merchandising opportunities were numerous; the brand equity building potential was great. But would management do the right thing?

After it was decided that the product introduction would remain in a 16 oz. jar with a half-pound of quality meat, the key to its success or failure was clearly going to be about marketing strategy and planning. If the size and quality of the new product were not to be compromised, then we needed to give the consumer a good enough reason to try it at perhaps even a higher than suggested retail price of $3.79. And the success of Rich & Meaty would be determined solely on our ability to achieve high trial rates in the marketplace. The plan, therefore, had to be clear about defining its MUST WIN BATTLES.

Must Win Battles:

#1 Ragu Rich & Meaty would be the first Ragu product to extend "out of aisle." It would be the challenge of sales and marketing to secure in-store placements for Ragu Rich & Meaty away from the slow traffic pasta aisle, i.e., around the perimeter of the store in the fresh meat sections, in the bread aisle for Sloppy Joes, snack aisle as a meat dip.

#2 A major advertising and promotional campaign would support the product's differentiation, providing the consumer with ideas for new ways to use this Ragu sauce. TV advertising was used to create consumer demand. In-store promotions were utilized to enhance brand visibility. Combined, this created the consumer *"pull"* in the traditional *push/pull* marketing mix.

And together, the first two must-win-battles were critical to supporting the product's reason-for-being (creating the retail customer *"push"*).

#3 The brand positioning for Ragu is *"Everyday Ingenuity."* And this positioning led to the promotional platform: *"Just Hanging Out."* When there's a gathering of people (friends, family, fellow sports fans, etc.), Ragu is the food product to serve—because with Ragu comes the Core Value—*Versatility*—you can prepare so many different snacks and easy meals. You get my drift.

Combining all three must-win-battles, a promotional tie-in was created linked to the National Football League®, and in particular to tailgating events, and related food recipes. John Madden was the bigger-than-life campaign spokesman used in prominently placed in-store point-of-purchase displays, as well as in print magazine ads. He acted as the catalyst for the *"How Do You Ragu?*™*"* Recipe Sweepstakes—a recipe contest encouraging consumers to submit creative uses for Ragu Rich & Meaty, with a first prize trip to the NFL Pro Bowl® in Hawaii.

Additionally, Comedian Dom DeLuise was used in public relations with promotional videos demonstrating unique recipe ideas. Ragu Rich & Meaty was the catalyst to Ragu's new association with *Versatility* as the brand's *Core Value*. After all, it's just like our call to action challenge for new recipes said to consumers, "How do you Ragu?"

Back to basics—The number one challenge here was to reduce price as a discriminating factor as to why this brand would be chosen. We wanted Mr. and Mrs. "Harvey & Harriet Lunchpail" to buy Ragu Rich & Meaty because they desired this product, not because it was an equally priced alternative to their usual jar sauce. Knowingly, this would not be easy at a $3.79 or higher price point in store.

But here's the real kicker. Remember that the big win for Ragu Rich & Meaty was to begin a brand extension campaign that promoted Ragu sauces for other uses. In other words, the purpose of this new product was to launch new life into the entire Ragu line. But here's what happened. Accounting dictated the pricing. The head bean counters insisted that the success of Ragu Rich & Meaty, like any other Ragu product, must be measured on the merits of its own profit and loss statement. These mandates caused marketing to lose control of the bigger strategy. The brand marketing team lost its ability to creatively introduce this first alternative use product—to achieve greater trial—to achieve the ultimate goal of increasing overall brand equity—to get the consumer to think positively about Ragu again.

Now, here comes the great *'What If?'* What if Ragu Rich & Meaty was introduced in a promotionally-priced trial size, with a major alternative-use advertising campaign to support its out-of-aisle, in-store placement? That way, marketing could make the strong case that Ragu Rich & Meaty should be perceived company-wide as a marketing promotional or merchandising tool rather than as a new product having to stand on its own, with its own P&L. And it should be treated as such. Its success would not have been measured as a traditional stand-alone product, with a forced 50 percent gross margin target dictating the price point at retail. Instead, wouldn't it now be a line-item expense under marketing costs? Something worth consideration and debate, don't you think?

Here's the beauty of what might have been. The consumer is encouraged, through trial size and promotional pricing, to try Ragu Rich & Meaty. And because we know it needs to be all about the consumer, the quality of the product is right, and its packaging and distribution are right, so the Harvey and Harriet's of the world love the Ragu Rich & Meaty product. Therefore, they are willing to pay the high price of $3.79 or higher for the 16 oz. package jar size. In-store value-added promotions and advertising continue to put Ragu first in the minds of consumers who want simple, affordable ideas for quick and easy meals. Now, even the price of the basic Ragu line items can creep up. As the brand equity improves, as the result of successful innovation, like with Rich & Meaty, so does the ability to take sustainable price increases for gross margin growth.

Now, what happens? The entire Ragu product line experiences overall gross profit *dollar* increases. The increases are driven as the result of greater acceptance of the brand portfolio on the part of the brand's consumer base. Price as a discriminating factor as to why Ragu gets chosen is now REDUCED, thus the brand is better positioned to take further price increases going forward. This because the brand would be implementing such price increase moves from a position of strength in the market with both the consumer and the retailer. Now that would be a product line profit story business schools write case studies about.

Oh, and wouldn't my friend Dick be happy!

Chapter 4

Lesson Four — Pricing is a Brand Strategy Decision, Not a P&L Plug

"If You Build It, They Will Come."

— From the movie, *Field of Dreams*

So you're dreaming again. You're the marketing head honcho for the day. And lucky you, a new product is ready for market launch. You get to recommend the selling price. Easy now. You do all of the research, then determine what to charge based on your costs to produce and distribute, packaging and levels of promotion, right? Well, it is right if you're asking the finance department. But what about asking your self this question instead: What price SHOULD we charge in support of the overall brand position? Now you're looking more like brand czar for the day!

What is the overall brand about? Or what is this new product within an existing brand about? Is it like *Suave®*, a product line that successfully calls itself a competitive quality performer at a lower price? Or is it a *Jaguar®*, a brand that flaunts its high price tag without talking much about performance or handling or quality. It's more about style.

In either case—establishing a lower than competition or top of its class price point—you will be sure to meet with substantial objections, and not just from finance and accounting. Wait until you have to inform the sales team that they're going to market with a product that sells at a price 30 percent higher than its closest competitor, and no, there isn't all that much of a difference in the product. The challenge is to convince them that pricing is an integral part of brand positioning.

25

And it WILL sell at 30 percent higher than its competitor, simply because your marketing plan is right on target.

CASE STUDY: *ABSOLUT® VODKA*

Critical Insight: *Absolut® Vodka* made the essential decision at the beginning—it would position itself as a *Fashion* brand, intentionally high priced, intentionally pretentious—exclusive to a few.

Marketing Strategy: Appeal to the young, hip market with creative, "hot" ads that scream: *"I know what's hot. I've made it. I'm too cool for old brand vodkas—even if I can't tell the difference drinking it mixed, straight-up, or shaken, not stirred."*

REWIND

Before any of the award winning ads, before vodka martinis became more popular than the more traditional gin martini, and before most people even bothered their bartender with a "called" vodka brand, the marketing heads at Absolut had made the one most important decision that led them to success. They established a single-minded brand position. Then, they followed through, consistently, from concept to packaging to promotion to pricing.

The Absolut brand's market was clear: young, up and coming professionals and trend-setters. Equally as clear was how they would drive this market: unique packaging (the bottle), marketing driven with high fashion, trend-setting print ads and the high price tag to support its high-end place in the market. Absolut was to make vodka the coolest drink to have and to hold, with a call for Absolut a virtual declaration that at the other end of that martini glass was someone who *"had arrived."*

In the early entry years in the U.S. market, Absolut outspent *Smirnoff®*, the industry leader, at least two to one in print media buys. And they could do this because of their extraordinarily high profit margin. Think about this. Smirnoff has to sell twice as many cases of vodka as Absolut to make the same profit.

This was a calculated exercise in spending a lot up front to roll the brand out quickly and with a huge sense of presence. The strategic reason? Because the marketing geniuses behind the rollout knew they had only a six-month window once it was launched. Then, as sure as vodka is a clear, tasteless, not-too-distinguishable liquid, the competitors would use all of their market leverage to launch competing, high-end products.

So Absolut was launched in a unique bottle, with a major marketing campaign aimed at establishing a clear image, with unmistakable visual recognition. The advertising revolved around the image of the distinctive Absolut bottle. A halo above the bottle, and its simple, yet effective, copy headline, *"Absolut Perfection,"* became legendary. So avant-garde was the advertising campaign that an entire coffee table book was created of Absolut print ads.

Meanwhile, at the hottest clubs and bars, price had not only become a non-factor in choosing a vodka, but higher price was part of the allure, part of the status image that was becoming synonymous with the Absolut brand.

Has Absolut become a short and sweet case study? Absolutely! Because when you get it right the first time, there's not much more to say then perhaps this is a classic case study … in *"Brand Perfection!"*

Chapter 5

Lesson Five — Low Hanging Fruit Always Tastes Great

"Discovery consists of looking at the same thing as everyone else and thinking something different."

—Albert Szent-Gyorgi

American companies spend hundreds of millions every year developing new products. And they continue to do this year after year even though, on average, eight out of every ten new products will fail. Some because they are ahead of their time, others because their marketing campaigns don't communicate effectively with their target audience, still others because they can't achieve the optimal level of distribution or visibility (i.e., in-store shelf space) they need for successful retail launch.

So what's the alternative? Look for the *low-hanging fruit.* Look hard at your product. See what everyone else sees. Then, see the potential for something else.

There are many ways to grow a brand's market share without introducing a grand new product—without having to re-create Mecca. Consider the example of packaging in innovation. The introduction of an innovative new package can drive brand switching and can be responsible for significant growth in market share, and almost always without the enormous cost and time associated with other more taxing new product development initiatives.

Examples—*Skippy® Peanut Butter* and *Hellmann's® Real Mayonnaise* introduced their market leader brands in a squeeze bottle. Kids and moms loved it. The convenience factor and the new attention it brought to the same reliable product, generated immediate brand switching and helped ensure continued brand loyalty.

Plastic bottles for beer and spirits (liquors) are another example. For example, the plastic bottle has helped *Budweiser*® to further increase its share of the market, especially in the out-of-home market. The consumer's simple choice of plastic over glass for the seasonal outdoor gathering—i.e., tailgate party, concert, barbeque, is enough for such consumers to switch brands in a heartbeat, often without a second thought.

There are a great number of opportunities hanging right in front of us if we can stop trying to hit those long home runs all the time and focus on driving the very efficient and effective singles and doubles. It's great to think long ball like Barry Bonds, but it's perhaps more realistic to perform speed ball like Ichiro Suzuki.

CASE STUDY: *SMIRNOFF® VODKA*

Critical Insight: The *Smirnoff*® brand is the largest selling vodka brand in the world, with case sales near doubling its nearest rival in the U.S. market alone. However, the brand had eroded as an image brand. It had weak identity in the minds of the U.S. consumer—especially among the younger, trend-setting consumers that frequent the most hip bars in major cities across the U.S. It was largely kept off the back bar and was hidden in the well (if in the bar at all), where no-name and old reliable brands are readily used but not called for by name. Bartenders weren't hearing yells for a Smirnoff martini over a three-customer-deep crowd.

The Challenge: Create interest in an old brand. Make it young again. Create a strong enough demand that Smirnoff resumes a space on the back bars of America, and in off-shelf displays in wine and spirit stores.

REWIND

A single price point increase on Smirnoff Vodka was worth over $15 million in increased gross profit contribution in a given year. So finding the low hanging fruit here was the most logical strategy, as long as the quality or effectiveness of the change in marketing strategy was strong enough to sustain the much sought after price increase.

When I first arrived at Smirnoff, I did the usual introductions and insight-gathering sessions with the top executives. One of the earliest meetings I remember with the VP of Sales was a lunch we set up specifically to address the challenges he saw then and moving forward.

I brought with me the single page print ad that had introduced the new Citrus lemon-lime flavored vodka, Smirnoff's first attempt at entering the hot, growing new flavored vodka market. The ad was beautiful. It featured a one-liter bottle of *Smirnoff Citrus Twist*® lemon-lime flavored vodka, only the bottle appeared to be physically twisted—a computer-generated twist on the new product's identity.

Ted (Sales VP) and I sat and talked for a while. Mostly I listened. Smirnoff had fallen off the radar screen with bartenders, according to sales, and it was a major challenge to figure out how to get it displayed once again in high image bars and restaurants where new products were most often sampled—leading the way to tremendous gains in retail liquor store distribution and sales.

I listened for what seemed a long time. Then I said, *"Ted, what would it do for sales if we actually brought this Citrus Twist to market in a twisted glass bottle, like in this ad?"* With the speed of a lightening bolt that had just jarred his frontal lobes, he answered with one word: *"Tremendous."* He went on, *"We'd have tremendous success getting a unique bottle like that on the back bars,"* he said, *"without a doubt."*

Frustratingly, but not surprisingly, it took almost a year to make it happen. I started with Jim, VP for product packaging development. *"No way,"* he said. *"You can't twist a bottle and then get it down the production line. It can't be done."* And there came the magic words that can instantly put me on overdrive to solution. *"It can't be done,"* is like the ultimate truth or dare challenge. As long as I have the confidence, as I did with the twisted bottle, then there must be a way, the word *"can't"* is simply a temporary, misguided obstacle.

Here's what we knew. Value-added (flavoring) should mean higher price. And further, in this case, Smirnoff Citrus Twist had a better chance of succeeding as a higher priced choice to the regular Smirnoff 80 proof non-flavored product if the packaging was unique. In fact, I believed this was critical to making the brand attractive to a younger audience, who look to the displayed brands on the back bar to call for a brand. And we knew that the new citrus flavor could be more profitable, not just because of its higher price, but because it could be packaged with less alcohol. The small drop from 80 to 70 proof would lower alcohol taxes and actually improve the taste. Less alcohol meant a better tasting, less sharp flavored vodka product. And, as we describe in detail later in this book in chapter eight, exhibit 8-11, this fit just fine into the Smirnoff brand promise, *"Smirnoff Accents the Taste; Never Disguises the Flavor."* The challenge was how to get the job done.

What happened next is a good lesson in planning. If we were to find a solution and convince the powers that be that it can be and should be done, we needed a strategic plan with a team approach. We had invested the time in developing a strong brand creative brief when I arrived. It made it clear what was to be our brand positioning platform, our messages, our objectives and strategic emphasis. So I took this model, tweaked it, and transformed it into a "creative packaging development brief." Now we would have a written road map, an integrated packaging brand team of players (from marketing, sales, packaging and manufacturing) who were committed to clear objectives—committed to finding a reasonable way to produce and bring to market a one-liter size twisted bottle, with just the right new look for a Smirnoff flavor product entry.

On the packaging brand team were a packaging manager, a manufacturing/production manager, a sales manager and the brand manager for flavors. Together they would research, test, present and ultimately design the new twisted bottle. But even with a strong team plan recommendation, one more element was critical to its success. The commitment level of each member of the team had to be tied to the success of the task at hand. So each team player had built into his and her individual annual performance evaluation the objectives, priorities and measurable success criteria associated with bringing the twisted bottle concept to reality, including the ultimate success of its presence on back bars.

And, in the final analysis, the results speak for itself,

Today, with several flavors, each presented in a unique twisted bottle, Smirnoff has relatively quickly regained its once lost presence in the bar scene. Other, longer-term innovations were also tried in the ready-to-drink or RTD segment ultimately leading to the highly successful ready-to-drink innovation branded *Smirnoff Ice®*. For Smirnoff, all new product efforts were designed in support of a strategy to capture a new, younger target market.

Together, a series of initiatives—low-hanging fruit initiatives—were instrumental in reinventing the Smirnoff brand, rejuvenating it for a whole new generation of spirit drinkers.

Like Ichiro hitting singles and doubles with men in scoring position, Smirnoff played speed ball and drove the singles and doubles it needed to get fast results—it wasn't always pretty, but in the end, the market share leader successfully defended its position.

Chapter 6

Lesson Six — Those that Carry the Wood Get to Sit by the Fire

Brand Strategies for managing within the Realities of Today's Budget & Time Constraints

"... The key characteristic of a marketing general is flexibility. It's not glamorous and it's not always recognized as a virtue, but no military general has been successful without it. A general must be flexible enough to adjust the strategy to the situation and not vice versa."

—Excerpt from the book *Marketing Warfare*,
by Al Ries and Jack Trout, 1986

If you can find ten corporate-level marketing executives who have been in the same position for the past decade or so, ask them this question: *"what is the most significant change they've had to adjust to as business is conducted in the new millennium?"*

If their answer isn't that long-term targets have been redefined from several years out to the next three months, they've either been on the golf course more than in their office or they're paying someone else a lot of money to pay attention for them to what's really going on in the business world.

A clear majority of publicly traded companies have experienced metamorphic change in the past decade. With one of the largest stock market "corrections" in U.S. history still in recent memory (2000-2002), investors remain nervous. Yes, some of this was driven by the economic aftermath of 9-11, but much was also the result of the Dot Com bust of the late '90's, early 2000's. The stock market's volatility has led to a clear change in management's approach to meeting its financial targets. Today, financial targets are managed almost strictly to quarterly results and a far shorter-term horizon for stock price appreciation and fluctuation. Managing for long-term results appears to have left corporate America with the 25-year service gold watch. Said differently, the message sent to publicly traded companies from the Wall Street investment community was clear—*"meet or exceed your quarterly profit targets or expect sharp declines in your company's market capitalization."*

This phenomenon has profound implications on the marketing function. More critical then ever is how marketing executives evaluate their brand portfolios, including strategic options, tactical priorities and budget allocation.

Historically, brand managers were charged with building brand equity for the longer term, typically three to five years out at least. Rarely would a marketer side for short-term sales or profit contribution at the expense of long-term brand health. But clearly the rules of engagement have changed. Marketers are expected to identify incremental revenue drivers and profit enhancements through cost reductions on a quarterly, if not monthly, basis. Budgets for brand investment are tightening; thus limited funds must be made to work harder and yes faster.

Long-term has become short-term and short-term has become the next monthly internal operating committee report, followed by the next quarterly report out to the Street.

But does today's reality have to mean the end of brand investment for equity-building in the long-term?

No. Today's reality simply challenges the marketer to fine-tune their strategic approach to managing brand equity. In fact, today's reality requires a new approach—one that builds on a brand's strength, identifies priority strategies and tactics within prioritized budgets, and within the context of corporate targets, quarterly time frames and the brand's competition.

A brand's future is NOW!

Brand success stories will be defined by the marketer's ability to stay focused on a very disciplined plan for allocating and managing brand budgets. But while the strategies should be dictated by a defined model for investment (see Chapter 7:

Brand Activation Matrix Strategy Model), it is ultimately the flexibility on the part of the marketer that will be the measure, and reward, of true success.

Wait, isn't that contradictory? Not at all. Think about it. As a brand marketer, you will be tested on your ability to be a team player, to make the necessary brand investment sacrifices that deliver the short-term profit results that are in keeping with your company's quarterly financial goals. You will be measured by how effectively you adhere to such shorter-term directives by fine-tuning your strategic approach to managing brand equity. So, your approach must be so well defined that it dictates your strategy. Yet your action plan must be flexible, one that can change with the challenges of short-term financial winds, and even the tropical storms.

For example, you can bet half your salary that you will be directed to cut your media investment in the back half of nearly any given fiscal year, in order to close profit contribution gaps. We've all been there, done that. So how does one overcome? It is critical that you have a contingency media and promotional plan that delivers against your brand equity building objectives, despite the reality of a lower media investment level. The key is that your compromised plan will still be directed by your undying commitment to a clear strategic approach.

You will know you are fortunate to have planned ahead; pre-empted management's directive from above to slash and burn on budgets. But to the boss, you will appear flexible, compromising and willing to sacrifice for the greater good of the company because despite the pressure to disinvest in the brand, you still were able to deliver ALL the results—brand equity as well as short-term incremental profits. If your employer is worth working for, the reward will be evident in positive performance evaluations, cash bonuses and your potential for greater, faster career advancement.

CASE STUDY: *MERCEDES BENZ®* *(courtesy of Lowe & Partners, New York)*

Given today's corporate realities, a new strategic approach is needed for successful brand marketing. Chapter 7 details a new brand equity tool to help outline specific workable strategies and action plans within a brand. Called the *Brand Activation Matrix Strategy Model*, it builds on a brand's strengths, while prioritizing budgets in favor of critical quarterly priorities.

The traditional approach to tightening budgets would be to identify which brands within a company warrant what level of budget support. But the new *Brand Activation Matrix* goes much further. It identifies priority strategies and tactics for individual brands, relative to competitive standing. It provides a strategic platform for putting brand equity to work in today's shorter-term, deliver results now, world.

While the leadership team at *Mercedes Benz®* likely had not yet heard of the *Brand Activation Matrix* when they launched the development and introduction of the C-Class, it is a classic success story of a new product strategy driven by an analysis of a brand's *relative brand equity* and *relative market share*. Ultimately, the C-Class fulfilled the need for broader distribution of the Mercedes Benz brand. It built on the strength of its high brand equity (compared to other automobiles that would compete with the new C-Class). Mercedes invested heavily in development and marketing of a new product that more people could afford, and more of their target audience (particularly women) would be driven to drive (no pun intended).

Critical Insight: Historically, Mercedes Benz was clearly defined by its core, loyal users as *dignified, trustworthy, exclusive* and *confident*. But consumers of the 1990s wanted something different; they wanted *dynamic, approachable* and *fun*. Mercedes Benz was viewed by younger audiences as *"arrogant"* and *"old fashion,"* particularly when compared to the new Japanese import offerings at the time—*Acura®, Lexus®, Infinity®.* Simply put, relevance to a new, younger and more female consumer could not be achieved with the current Mercedes Benz mix of products.

If Mercedes Benz had gone through Chapter 7's exercise of mapping itself within the *Brand Activation Matrix*, it would find itself classified as a *Hide & Seek* Brand. Brands that fall into this category are not easily accessible by those consumers who want them (explained by their low relative market share) even though these target consumers appear highly interested in the products (as evidenced by high relative brand equity).

REWIND

From 1966 to 1986, Mercedes-Benz was the pre-eminent luxury car in the U.S. market, with few challenges. It could build a car the way it wanted, including every bell and whistle, and charge its customers a premium price. The result was over 20 years of sustained growth, peaking during the boom of the 1980s at sales of 100,000 automobiles in 1986.

However, by 1987, the competitive and economic landscape significantly changed. Almost simultaneously, several key events had a dramatic effect on the Mercedes Benz market:

- implementation of the luxury import tax
- a forecasted economic recession or downturn in consumer confidence
- sea change in consumer attitudes away from status symbols and toward practicality

and perhaps most telling,

- entrance of Japanese luxury competitors

By 1992, Mercedes Benz sales had plummeted 38 percent over an eight year period of time, bottoming out at about 60,000 units (down from a high of 100,000 in 1986). The challenge was clear—to enhance the brand image, making it more relevant to new customers, without disenfranchising their current high loyalty customers.

The single-minded goal: *Reverse the sales decline while making the brand more relevant to a younger consumer.*

The product strategy was targeted and clear. Don't change what's working for the traditional Mercedes Benz customer. Instead, produce and market a new line of car that boldly whispers, *"gotta drive me"* to the younger, successful consumer, particularly women. Thus, the C-Class was born.

Built into the strategy was a new challenge for the brand marketing team. How do we make the engineering relevant in the new C-Class? Mercedes Benz was all about engineering ... *"Best Car in the World."* How would this translate into a more affordable, *"approachable class"* Mercedes Benz?

What did *"Best Car in the World"* mean to this new consumer? To the loyal Mercedes Benz customer and to the new target customer alike, it meant *luxury, the best engineering, safety.* But wasn't it also a pleasure to drive? So it would be believable for a new, more affordable Mercedes Benz to be *Stylish and Fun* to drive.

Fun to drive, *Value, Safety* and *Style.* These became synonymous with the C-Class. The new branding led to the evolution of *"Best Car in the World"* to *"Best Car for Me,"* which provided the creative direction for the high impact media campaign that would elevate the Mercedes Benz brand to a new level of consumer stardom, almost overnight.

Several highly visible, tremendously successful advertising commercial executions become classic illustrations of the power of a clear marketing strategy. One 30 second television commercial shows the new C-Class in a beautiful country setting, with dream-like imaging. The visual is striking. The only sound is a vocal of Janice Joplin singing:

> ♫ *Oh Lord won't you buy me a Mercedes Benz*
> *My Friends all drive Porches … I must make amends*
> *Worked hard all my lifetime … No help from my friends*
> *So Lord, won't you buy me a Mercedes Benz … That's It* ♫

Another 60 second television commercial execution, similar in its high-image feel and effect, featured the famous lyrics, written by German composer Friedrich Holländer, with English version by Sammy Lerner, of the song *"Falling in Love Again."* Marlene Dietrich made this song famous in the 1930 film *"The Blue Angel."* The song acted as the Mercedes Benz brand's umbrella big theme anthem-like message. If you haven't seen the commercial, just imagine the magic and emotion as the song's lyrics ring through the airwaves and are supported with black and white images showing the evolution of the Mercedes Benz car models over several decades. One verse, of the *"Falling in Love Again"* lyrics, goes like this:

> ♫ *Falling in love again … Never wanted to*
> *What am I to do … I can't help it*
> *Love's always been my game … Play it how I may*
> *I was made that way … I can't help it* ♫

Both the *Janis* and *Falling in Love Again* executions were relatively very expensive television commercials to produce, yet exclusive to the Mercedes Benz brand. The overall campaign delivered very own-able ads that broke through clutter and grabbed your attention. Ads that pulled on your heart strings and sold product! And that is what big brands do—what leadership brands do!

Mercedes Benz hit a homerun with the C-Class. Sales and brand equity rose monumentally:

- Mercedes Benz car sales rose 47 percent from 1992 to 1996, from 62,000 units to just under 90,100. And, at this time, an increase to 125,000 units was projected by 1999. That's an increase of 101 percent from 1992!
- The medium age of a Mercedes driver decreased by five years.
- Women's ranking of Mercedes Benz drastically improved for image and acceptability, equal to or higher than among their male counterparts.

Mercedes Benz is the success story of true marketing czars. Yes, award winning media campaigns are nice to have under your professional belt. But this win was all about strategy. When a brand team and ultimately senior management utilize the right road map for program prioritization and budget allocation—in this case leaping into a major investment in new product development—profit targets can more often be met and exceeded, even in times of economic distress and shrinking overall budgets.

In one's heart of hearts, I think even Janice Joplin would have been proud.

PART 2

New Tools for the Trade —
Meaningful Brand Planning

Chapter 7

Lesson Seven—Where Have All the Brand Strategists Gone?

Introducing the Brand Activation Matrix Strategy Model

A Matrix Model for Outlining Workable Brand Strategies within
Realities of Budget Constraints and Time On Return Expectations.

"Difficulties Mastered are Opportunities Won."

—Sir Winston Churchill

SITUATION ANALYSIS

The central message of this chapter dovetails from today's reality of how publicly-traded companies are managing their businesses in lieu of increasing investor volatility. As companies today move more and more to managing their businesses to quarterly results, marketing executives, in particular, need to change their approach to how they evaluate their brand portfolios in terms of strategic options, tactical priorities and budget allocation. What is new and useful in this chapter is the introduction of the *Brand Activation Matrix* strategy model—one that builds on the Boston Consulting Group pioneering work known as the Business Portfolio or *Growth-Share Matrix Model*.

This chapter is designed primarily as a blueprint guide to help the professional marketing executive—Chief Marketing Officers, V.P. Marketing, Brand Directors and Brand Managers. However, the proposed theories, guidance and resulting workable model and related information is also useful to any senior executive with influence over the marketing strategies and/or marketing budgets of the company (i.e., CEO's, COO's, GM's, CFO's).

45

Today's Reality

As businesses entered the new millennium, most publicly traded companies experienced metamorphic change in how they are structured organizationally, how they budget resources for supporting customer segments and how their current shareholders, and the investment community overall, assess the company's business model in relation to that stakeholder's own return on investment or ROI expectations. In fact, managing for "long-term" results is a thing of the past; overtaken by increased volatility in the financial markets. Recall from chapter six's discussion regarding how we experienced the largest stock market correction in our nation's recent history just this past 2000-2002. This "nervousness" or volatility on the part of stock market investors has led to a clear change in management's approach to meeting its financial targets—one that manages almost strictly to quarterly results and shorter-term horizon stock price appreciation/fluctuations.

The above phenomena may be having profound implications on how marketing executives evaluate their brand portfolios in terms of strategic options, tactical priorities and budget allocation. Historically, brand managers were charged with building brand equity over the longer-term, say a minimum of three and up to five to seven years; rarely siding for short-term sales or profit contribution gains at the expense of long-term brand health. Today, the rules of engagement have clearly changed. Marketers are expected to identify incremental revenue drivers and profit enhancements through cost reductions, on a quarterly, if not monthly, basis. Long-term has become short-term and short-term has become the next monthly operating committee report out internally; next quarterly report out to Wall Street's investment community.

Although on the surface this would appear to be the beginning of the end for investing in brands, all is not lost when it comes to building brand equity. Marketers can more effectively adhere to such shorter-term directives by fine-tuning their strategic approach to managing brand-equity. However, a new strategic approach is needed—one that builds on the brand's strengths, while prioritizing budgets in favor of addressing critical priority/within quarter issues.

Building on Proven Models

The Boston Consulting Group (BCG) pioneering work known as the Growth-Share Business Portfolio Matrix Model presented managers with a systematic approach to giving priority to individual brands across the company or strategic business unit's total brand portfolio.

Cash Cows were used to generate profits to fuel *Stars* and possibly *Question Marks*. *Dogs* were abandoned and overall a company was better positioned to determine which brands warranted what level of budget support ($).

Once it was determined how much ($) each individual brand was allocated for support, brand managers were then charged with crafting strategies and designing action plans, that make use of that allocated budget support, in addressing the brand's key issues and challenges—all with an eye toward building brand equity over the long-term.

Exhibit 7-1: The BCG Business Portfolio Matrix

Growth - Share Matrix

	High		
	Stars	**Question Marks**	
	Situation: Cash Using	*Situation:* Cash Using or Cash Trap	
Market Growth Rate	*Strategy:* Build	*Strategy:* Build, Harvest or Divest	
	Tactics: Highest Investment	*Tactics:* New Venture R&D Investment	
	Cash Cows	**Dogs**	
	Situation: Fuel for Growth	*Situation:* Cash Trap	
	Strategy: Hold or Harvest	*Strategy:* Harvest or Divest	
	Tactics: Steady Reinvestment	*Tactics:* Selective Pruning or Rejuvenation	
	Low		

High   Relative Market Share   Low

Exhibit 7-1 above shows how the Growth-Share Matrix provides an *across brands* blueprint for sizing-up a strategic business unit's or SBU strategic opportunities. Whilst the BCG model helped to prioritize brands for support, a new, complementary strategic approach is needed to help outline specific workable strategies and action plans *within brand* in meeting today's reality.

Putting Brand Equity to Work

Exhibit 7-2 below introduces a new Brand Equity—Market Share Strategy Matrix Model that identifies priority strategies and tactics for individual brands relative to competitive issues. Coined the *Brand Activation Matrix*, this model provides a strategic platform for putting Brand Equity to work, given today's reality.

Here, we define brand equity as the *set of assets* including, but not limited to, *name awareness, loyalty, perceived quality* and *image attributes* that are linked to the brand and, in effect, add value to the product or service being offered. In a modeling sense, brand equity can be measured as a function *(f)* of:

- *Awareness/Name Recognition*—measured by top-of-mind or unaided recall
- *Loyalty*—combination of brand preference ratings and resistance to compromise
- *Quality*—defined as Value x Price
- *Image*—key attribute ratings other than Price
- *Distribution*—measured by availability (i.e. all-commodity volume referred to as ACV) and visibility (in-store attractiveness through merchandising)

In measuring a brand's equity, the resulting beneficiaries remain to be Consumers who seek *convenience, confidence* and overall product or service *satisfaction*, as well as the Company itself which seeks *higher margins* (through more premium pricing), *trade leverage* when building channel relationships and *budget efficiencies* when allocating scarce investment resources.

In the model, the term *relative brand equity* refers to measuring a brand's equity relative to that brand's nearest competitor, as defined by market share. Hence, the inputs of *unaided recall, preference, resistance to compromise, price/value, image attributes, all-commodity volume (ACV),* and *in-store presence* when measured and modeled for an overall brand equity rating, such rating is then compared to the overall brand equity rating of that brand's nearest competitor.

Likewise, market share is defined as a function (f) of *brand loyalty* and *distribution* (combination of breadth and depth) with the term *relative market share* following the BCG Matrix Model's definition of nearest competitor.

Exhibit 7-2: The Brand Activation Matrix Strategy Model

Brand Activation Matrix

	Low	High
High Relative Brand Equity **Low**	*Hide & Seeks* *Issue:* Distribution *Strategy:* Increase Visibility *Tactics:* Media, Sampling, Merchandising, NPD *Lonely Hearts* *Issue:* Product Relevance *Strategy:* Increase Category Price Sensitivity *Tactics:* Promotions	*Attention Getters* *Issue:* Market Saturation *Strategy:* Expand Usage/Reach *Tactics:* Brand Extensions, Franchising, Global Expansion *Daydreamers* *Issue:* Lack of Differentiation *Strategy:* Build Image to Decrease Price Sensitivity *Tactics:* New Creative Campaign/Activation Platform

Relative Market Share

Sizing-up the Brand

Each quadrant within the *Brand Activation Matrix* represents the current state of the brand as defined by that brand's key issues and challenges. Thus, a brand that falls into the quadrant defined by *high relative brand equity—low relative market share* is a brand faced with a distribution challenge that can only be addressed by improving that brand's visibility to the target audience.

For a brand falling into the quadrant defined by *high relative brand equity—high relative market share* is a brand likely challenged by market saturation; thus seeking to expand its usage and/or reach.

In the case of a brand fitting within the quadrant defined by *low relative brand equity—high relative market share*, the challenge becomes one of clearly defining points of differentiation, typically to build image in order to decrease the price sensitivity inherent in commodity-like competitive sets.

Finally, for those brands defined by *low relative brand equity—low relative market share,* the key issue is one of relevance and a brand trying to compete from this quadrant will likely have to promote heavily in order to focus the target audience on price as the key discriminating factor as to why the brand should be in one's consideration set.

REAL-WORLD IMPLICATIONS

The central message can be applied in businesses today by offering marketers a very focused and disciplined approach to allocating and managing brand budgets. This short-term discipline is needed more than ever as the corporate community finds itself in an ever fluid climate of change due to shorter-term reviews of business results and the underlying need for strategic and tactical flexibility when managing brands and related budgets.

Putting the Model to Work

Each quadrant in the matrix acts as a strategic blueprint from which the brand manager can better focus limited resources in order to meet the top and bottom-line objectives outlined in today's reality. The brand manager gets the most out of the brand over a shorter period of time—quarterly, monthly, or both. In effect, each quadrant defines a given brand for what it is. Instead of trying to transform that brand into something other then what it currently is, the brand manager simply leverages his/her fading resources in a most focused way. It is this sharpened focus combined with the discipline to stay the course that enables the manager to successfully address the key competitive issues and drive incremental top-line revenue growth.

Does this mean that for example, brands fitting into the lower left quadrant and challenged with product relevance issues would never advertise? No. However, it does mean that advertising would certainly not be the first order of business in driving sales growth on those brands. Brands fitting this profile can be classified as *Lonely Heart* brands. Brands that are *Lonely Hearts* continuously struggle to get consumers' attention (low relative market share) and consumers do not appear to respond with a strong desire to seek them out as evidenced by low relative brand equity. A prudent brand manager will see this and push his/her brand team to allocate resources against quick sales wins via price-based promotions and greater trade marketing support. Examples might include brands that are declining, with little to no growth over several years, such as *Continental Tire®, Prell® Shampoo, ERA® Real Estate* and the former *Montreal Expos® Major League Baseball Team*. A potential implication or risk associated with a *Lonely Hearts* strategy is weak long-term viability. A brand lacking a clear, differentiated reason-for-being to its target audience may be doomed long-term even with an attractive short-term price point or trade effort.

Opposite of this are brands fitting into the upper right quadrant and thus challenged by facing a saturated marketplace. Such brands need to expand product uses, usage occasions or geographic reach, typically by developing brand extensions and/or expanding globally. Perhaps even franchising provides the platform for rapid geographic expansion. Brands fitting this profile can be classified as *Attention Getter* brands. Brands that are *Attention Getters* live in the limelight as consumers express high desirability for them (high relative brand equity) and they are readily available to these interested consumers as evidenced by high relative market share. The brand team should focus its energy and resources on developing line extensions, opening new markets through globalization and/or developing new uses and or usage occasions for the product. Examples might include successful, leader brands that have experienced high growth. Brands like *Nike®, Budweiser®, Gatorade®, Target®, Wal*Mart®, Disney®, Home Depot®, Dell®, Starbucks®* and *Arm & Hammer®*. A potential implication or risk associated with an *Attention Getter* strategy is brand dilution. A most valuable brand can quickly go from being extraordinary to ordinary if care is not taken.

In contrast, brands fitting into the lower right quadrant and thus challenged with a lack of differentiation need new, bold creative advertising communications and/or promotional campaign(s) as the first order of business in order to re-build image. Brands fitting this profile can be classified as *Daydreamer* brands. Brands that are *Daydreamers* are very much in demand, perhaps based on sheer distribution presence, as evidenced by high relative market share. However, these brands must seek to become something bigger/bolder, something more unique, and something that is clearly different as evidenced by their vulnerability due to their low relative brand equity versus key competition. The brand manager should push to ring-fence advertising campaign and media dollars, and own-able promotional or activation platforms while satisfying the quarterly quick win scenario for profit growth by materially reducing wasted or inefficient price-promotion and trade allowance support. Examples might include mature brands, typically *Cash Cows*, like *Smirnoff® Vodka, Ragu® Pasta Sauce, McDonald's®, Kmart®, Gallo® Wines* and *Century 21® Real Estate* (re-review Century 21 case study presented back in chapter one). A potential implication or risk associated with a *Daydreamer* strategy is that re-staging a brand is often difficult and quite often not believable to the target audience.

Opposite of this are brands fitting into the upper left quadrant and challenged with the need to gain wider distribution in order to increase its visibility to the target audience. Brands fitting this profile can be classified as *Hide and Seek* brands. Brands that are *Hide and Seeks* are often not easily accessible by those consumers who want them (low relative market share) even though these target consumers appear highly interested as evidenced by high relative brand equity. The brand manager can gain top-line sales growth by planning tactical programs that include greater media presence, in-store merchandising and/or sampling, as well as new product development efforts that aid in expanding distribution reach. Brand examples might include such high-end positioned luxury products as *Rolls Royce®, Gucci®, Prada®, Audemars Piguet® Fine Swiss Watches, Tiffany's®* and at one time *Mercedes Benz®* and *Cadillac®* (prior to these companies introducing the *Mercedes C-Class®* and *Cadillac CTS®* respectively which helped enable both brands to move to the more attractive *Attention Getter* quadrant). A potential implication or risk associated with a *Hide and Seek* strategy is brand equity erosion which ultimately can lead to price and margin erosion.

For any of the above scenarios, the willingness and discipline to leverage budgets more efficiently leads to more effective return on investment. Savvy brand managers know that many in senior management tend to view budgets, not as investment opportunities, but rather as costs—"Costs" that can be avoided in the near term whenever necessary. Thus, when the brand team utilizes the *Brand Activation Matrix* as the road-map for program prioritization and budget allocation, there is an excellent chance that stretch quarterly sales and profit targets can be met even in times of shrinking budgets.

Yes the *Brand Activation Matrix* is a roadmap for program prioritization and thus budget allocation, but more than this, as was the case with Century 21 illustrated back in chapter one, it is the insurance policy that you are doing the right things to meet stretch quarterly sales and profit targets, given the brand's known key attributes.

So the brand team that utilizes the *Brand Activation Matrix* has a built-in confidence tool, keeping them so appropriately targeted that they are well positioned for whatever budget "corrections" are to come. And in doing so, you have an excellent chance of being successful, even in times of seemingly never-ending "frozen funds," budget cuts and/or budget redirects.

Chapter 8

Lesson Eight — Single-Minded Brand Positioning Means Never Having to Say You're Sorry

Differentiating Tools for Brand Architecture: the Positioning Pyramid Model, the Brand Essence and the Brand Promise as a Business Proposition

"An invasion of armies can be resisted, but not an idea whose time has come."

—Victor Hugo

What is brand positioning and why is this concept so important to a strategy for building brand equity? It's really quite simple—brand positioning is THE PLACE in the customer's mind that YOU WANT TO OWN. In fact, brand positioning is a lot like *True Love*—It's all about *Sacrifice!* You've got to give something up in order to gain something. Recall the examples from chapter one:

Volvo® = *safety*	Volvo ≠ style & performance
Smirnoff® = *mixability*	Smirnoff ≠ fashion
Dove® = *moisturizers*	Dove ≠ purity
Six Flags® = *thrill*	Six Flags ≠ family fun
Ivory® = *purity*	Ivory ≠ deodorant soap
Head & Shoulders® = *fights dandruff*	Head & Shoulders ≠ smooth & silky

In each of the cases above, the brand had to give up some position in order TO OWN another position—a better position RELATIVE TO COMPETITION.

53

To be most effective—to have the greatest return on investment—positioning must be:

1. Single-minded
2. Own-able
3. Defendable

And, on these three principles there can be NO COMPROMISE!
(Note: This is the only exclamation point in this book that is preceded by ALL CAPS. So read it again, it's that important.)

Now that you've got that, REALLY got it, we are ready to move on. Because the first step any brand marketer should take when stepping into a new company or to manage a new brand, or to reevaluate an existing brand, is to create a brand positioning platform using the model in this chapter. But creating a brand positioning platform that is not single-minded, not own-able, not defendable will be an exercise in futility. It must be, in one word, BELIEVABLE.

Developing the brand architecture requires several inputs—brand benefits, customer insights and descriptors of the brand's personality. Exhibit 8-1 below illustrates how the brand architecture is fully developed and includes the model inputs, milestones and resulting outcomes.

Exhibit 8-1: Brand Architecture — Modeling Inputs and Milestones

Developing the Brand Architecture

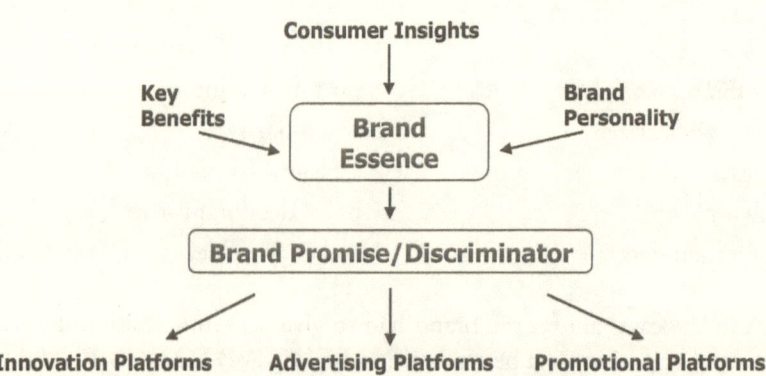

The architecture can then be fully constructed into the brand's positioning strategy by utilizing any of a number of brand positioning development models. I prefer to use the traditional Brand Positioning Pyramid Model. Why? Because this tool is an excellent way to gain focus and maintain discipline. In effect, it is forced sacrifice. Here, we drive to effectively build a brand positioning platform that truly works—that differentiates the brand in the most creative way and does this RELATIVE TO COMPETITON.

Here's how the pyramid model is designed to work ...

Start with a blank pyramid with a description of each level labeled on the outside of the pyramid model, as illustrated in exhibit 8-2 below.

Exhibit 8-2: Brand Positioning Platform—Pyramid Modeling Approach

Brand Positioning – Pyramid Model

How Are Brands Constructed?

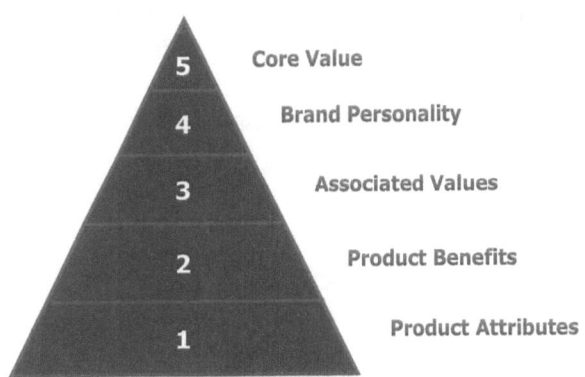

Now, starting at the bottom, identify the *Product or Physical Attributes* of the brand, followed by the *Product or Rational Benefits*, followed by the *Associated Values or Emotional Benefits*. Now, work up to descriptors of the *Brand Personality*. Now Stop! If there isn't one word that immediately comes to mind as the brand's *Core Value or Brand Essence* think about it carefully. The importance of *Core Value* cannot be underestimated. It will be your grounding point to which everything in your marketing will be measured; it is this *Brand Essence* that will evolve into the *Brand Promise* that will act as the foundation for a business proposition and will drive everything from *messaging* to *media strategies* and *promotion*, to *co-branding*

opportunities, and ultimately *pricing* decisions as well as *new product development* strategies.

To illustrate how the model works, consider a brand example using *Marlboro®* as illustrated in exhibit 8-3 below *(note: The Marlboro example is presented for learning purposes only and is not based on the brand's actual positioning strategy. With that said, given marketing expertise combined with some brand knowledge, this author would argue that the strategy presented is valid and worthy of consideration).*

In exhibit 8-3, notice how we move from the foundations of the brand which are physical in nature to the pinnacle of the brand which is emotional in nature. Remember, any competitor can match what your brand can physically do; it is the pinnacle or emotional component to your brand that is differentiating, and in fact, own-able. Said differently, any cigarette brand can claim to be satisfying; yet only one, *Marlboro ... provides 'Adventure.'*

Rule of thumb—the physical components of the positioning model should act as support to the emotional component and not vice-a-versa. The mistake many brand marketers make is that they advertise the brand's physical components (undifferentiating) over the emotional component (differentiating).

Exhibit 8-3: Marlboro Brand Positioning Platform

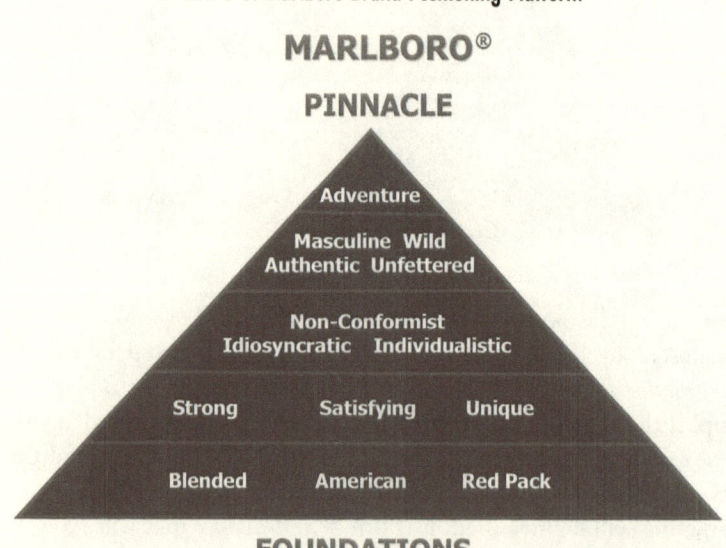

When it comes to identifying the brand's *Core Value* or *Brand Essence*, would you question the validity of any of these examples?

Marlboro® = *Adventure*

Haagen-Dazs® = *Indulgence*

Absolut® Vodka = *Fashion*

Keep this in mind—the basic approach to brand positioning is not to create something that is so different that it is not believable. Instead, positioning is about positively manipulating what's already viewed as the brand's unique personality. You want to bond with the customer (consumer) in a most focused and own-able way.

But how do we come up with these attributes? How do we know what should and/ or should not be included in the brand positioning pyramid model? This is where a brand positioning worksheet can be very useful. Exhibit 8-4 below illustrates the three key factor categories—*Key Drivers, Key Definers, Unowned Drivers*—that go into a useful brand positioning worksheet.

Exhibit 8-4: Brand Positioning Worksheet

Brand Positioning Worksheet

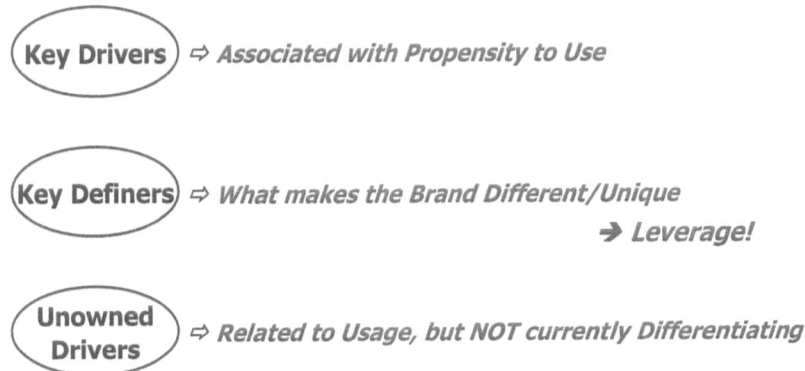

Key Drivers ⇨ Associated with Propensity to Use

Key Definers ⇨ What makes the Brand Different/Unique
➜ Leverage!

Unowned Drivers ⇨ Related to Usage, but NOT currently Differentiating

What's most important to digest here is that the worksheet provides for a systematic way to get at answers fast when it comes to developing the pyramid model.

Here, the *Key Drivers* of the brand are those attributes that your brand Must Deliver against. These are the attributes that customers look for when they participate in the purchase decision of your brand's product category. Next, the *Key Definers* of the brand are those attributes that your brand Must Sell against. These are the attributes that truly differentiate the brand and you want to leverage this with potential customers. Finally, the *Unowned Drivers* of the brand represent those attributes that your brand Must Forget. Yes, I did say Must Forget. Why? Because these are the attributes that your brand fails to differentiate on, therefore, although they are attributes related to usage, your brand is not believable when leveraging against such attributes.

Exhibit 8-5 below illustrates the brand positioning worksheet using *Six Flags Theme Parks* as the example.

Exhibit 8-5: Six Flags Theme Parks Brand Positioning Worksheet

Six Flags® Theme Parks
Brand Positioning Worksheet

Key Drivers ⇨ *Associated with Propensity to Use*

⇨ *Rides/Attraction*	⇨ *Every Day/Any Day*
⇨ *Close-to-Home*	⇨ *Convenient/Good Value*
⇨ *Family Fun/Excitement*	

Key Definers ⇨ *What makes the Brand Different/Unique* → *Leverage!*

⇨ *Cutting Edge/State-of-Art Technology*	⇨ *Speed/Risk*
⇨ *Irreverent/Rebellious*	⇨ *Participative/Interactive*

Unowned Drivers ⇨ *Related to Usage, but NOT currently Differentiating*

⇨ *Passive*	⇨ *Vacation/Special Occasions*
⇨ *Sophisticated*	⇨ *Educational/Informational*
⇨ *Warm/Caring*	

Notice in exhibit 8-5 above what the brand needs to deliver against (Key Drivers), sell against (Key Definers) and flat-out forget (Unowned Drivers) as the brand positioning strategy will be developed.

Now that we have the attributes defined, we are now ready to develop our strategic positioning utilizing the Brand Positioning Pyramid Model. Exhibit 8-6 below illustrates the brand positioning platform for Six Flags Theme Parks. This is the platform from which evolved the *Core Value* of the Six Flags brand to be about *'THRILL.'*

Exhibit 8-6: Six Flags Theme Parks Brand Positioning Platform

What follows in Exhibit 8-7 below is the *Brand Promise* for Six Flags. Why do we need this? If you go back to earlier in this chapter when we illustrated the Brand Architecture in Exhibit 8-1, you will notice that there are two key milestones to developing the architecture. First is the Brand's *Essence*, often referred to as the brand's *Core Value* (in the case of Six Flags, this is *Thrill*). This *Core Value* or *Brand Essence* in and of itself is not a business proposition. That's where the milestone, the Brand's *Promise* (or Discriminator), comes into play. The *Brand Promise* acts as the business proposition from which we develop the creative brief (see chapter nine). This is the systematic and disciplined process that leads to ALL marketing initiatives, including advertising, promotions, publicity/PR and new product development platforms.

Exhibit 8-7: Six Flags Brand Promise

**Six Flags® Theme Parks
Brand Positioning Platform**

SIX FLAGS <u>PROMISE</u>

*"HEIGHTENS THE THRILL OF ANY RIDE OR ATTRACTION;
NEVER PRESENTS A PASSIVE OR DEPRIVATIONAL
ENVIRONMENT. "*

What follows are four more brand examples of very effective brand positioning platforms with related brand promises acting as the brand's basic business proposition—exhibit 8-8 is for *Volvo®*, exhibit 8-9 is for *Michelin®*, exhibit 8-10 is for *Century 21® Real Estate* and exhibit 8-11 is for *Smirnoff® Vodka (note: The Volvo and Michelin examples are presented for learning purposes only and are not based on either brand's actual positioning strategy. With that said, given marketing expertise combined with some brand knowledge, this author would argue that the strategies presented are valid and worthy of consideration).*

For *Smirnoff*, notice we have also included, for your review, another example with the brand positioning worksheet that led to the Smirnoff Positioning Platform.

Exhibit 8-8: Volvo Brand Positioning Platform and Brand Promise

Volvo®
Brand Positioning Platform

Safety	Core Value
Hard / Trustworthy Dependable / Tank-Like	Brand Personality
High Standards High Performance / Long Life Crash-Proof / High Quality	Associated Values
Comfort Security / Relaxation Commitment / Durability	Product Benefits
Steel Frame/Cage 3-Point Seat Belts/Restraint Systems / Air Bags Technology Energy-Absorbing Impact Zones	Product Attributes

VOLVO® <u>PROMISE</u>

"Minimizes the risk of injury with a road hazard; never jeopardizing the well-being of its passengers."

Exhibit 8-9: Michelin Brand Positioning Platform and Brand Promise

Michelin®
Brand Positioning Platform

Security — Core Value

Tough/Strong
Protector   In-Control
Guardian — Brand Personality

Long-Life   High Performance
Balance   Safety
High Quality — Associated Values

Weather-Proof / Minimal Wheel Spin
Puncture Resistant   Low Maintenance
Low Vibration — Product Benefits

Steel-Belted   "Wear-Bars" Gauge   Tubeless
Usable Tread   Casing Ply Material — Product Attributes

MICHELIN® <u>PROMISE</u>

"Fortifies the safety and performance of the ride experience; never increases the risk of a road hazard."

Exhibit 8-10: Century 21 Brand Positioning Platform and Brand Promise

CENTURY 21®
Brand Positioning Platform

Core Value — Tranquility

Brand Personality — Leader, Honest, Unpretentious, Down-to-Earth, Respectable, Dependable, Trustworthy

Associated Values — Information source, Personal control, Ease-in-process, Best option/service, Partnership, Results-oriented

Product Benefits — Market knowledge/familiarity, Professional guidance/advice, Convenience, Commitment

Product Attributes — # offices, # listings, # sales associates, Geographic coverage, Branded alliances, State-of-art technology

CENTURY 21® <u>PROMISE</u>

"Eliminates any Anxiety or Apprehension with the buying/selling experience; never compromising on service, product offerings, and fast results."

Exhibit 8-11: Smirnoff Brand Positioning Worksheet, Platform and Brand Promise

Smirnoff ® Brand Positioning Worksheet

Key Drivers ⇨ *Associated with Propensity to Use*

⇨ *Made in Russia*   ⇨ *Proud to Serve*
⇨ *History as Quality Product*   ⇨ *Order by Name*
⇨ *For Use In Bars/Restaurants*   ⇨ *Currently Popular*

Key Definers ⇨ *What makes the Brand Different/Unique* ➔ *Leverage!*

⇨ *Brand I Trust*   ⇨ *Suitable for Anytime*
⇨ *Dependable*   ⇨ *Good for Mixed Drinks*
⇨ *Serve at Big Party*

Unowned Drivers ⇨ *Related to Usage, but NOT currently Differentiating*

⇨ *Expensive & Worth It*   ⇨ *For Sophisticated People*
⇨ *Superior Quality*   ⇨ *Exciting*
⇨ *For Special Occasions*   ⇨ *Classy Bottle*
⇨ *Makes Me Feel Special*

Smirnoff® Vodka
Brand Positioning Platform

Exhibit 8-11 continued

SMIRNOFF® PROMISE

> **"ACCENTS THE TASTE OF ANYTHING THAT POURS; NEVER DISGUISES THE FLAVOR."**

The brand examples presented in exhibits 8-8 through 8-11 above provide case study scenarios demonstrating that in order for brand positioning to be most effective, you *must give something up in order to gain something*. Volvo's are not sold purely on the consumer's desire for *Safety*, yet it is *Safety* presented as the brand's *Core Value* that enables Volvo to enter that consumer's evoked set of brands under consideration for purchase. Michelin being about *Security* translates to advertising creative that suggests your family is at risk if your car does not have Michelin tires on it. Six Flags provides *Thrill*, whereas Disney® provides *Family Fun*. Big difference! And one which helps position Six Flags to be relatively price insensitive to a Teen target audience. This means the need for fewer discounts—thus driving greater gross margin. Finally, with over eighty percent of vodka-based drinks being mixed, Smirnoff can effectively compete for bartender acceptance against the higher-end, imports like *Absolut®, Ketel One®*, and *Grey Goose®*—brands that tend to be promoted for neat or undiluted consumption.

So again, why is Brand Positioning so important? As you can decipher from the examples above, it is because, when done right, positioning differentiates you IMMEDIATELY. Volvo is about *Safety*. Six Flags is about *Thrill*. Positioning starts to sell the brand in such a way that you do not have to launch into a lengthy explanation about what the brand is all about. Positioning provides for that *'Ah-Ha'* factor that leaves no room for confusion.

And when you translate your *Brand Essence* (or *Core Value*) into a well thought-out *Brand Promise*, you now have a business proposition from which everything, EVERYTHING must execute against or it should be considered off strategy. Smirnoff *Accents the Taste; Never Disguises the Flavor* as the brand's promise or business proposition enables Smirnoff to effectively compete against *Bacardi®*, a rum product that absolutely disguises the flavor. This creates promotional opportunities for Smirnoff that rum-based brands like Bacardi can not own. In this case, as a result of a well thought-out, differentiating *Brand Promise*, those promotional opportunities for Smirnoff are more easily justified to management along with the budget requirements that accompany them.

Here are some clear facts to consider and rules of engagement to live by when it comes to brand positioning.

- ✓ Strategy means making choices—your brand can't, I REPEAT CAN'T, be all things to all people. You must decide what you want your brand to stand for and build the brand architecture around this mission.

- ✓ Focus on ONE THING that matters most to Customers/Consumers. Carve-out a space that is relevant and is rooted in a meaningful benefit.

- ✓ Own a BIG promise and STAY CONSISTENT.

- ✓ Very critically scrutinize how your brand is different from competition. Having a DIFFERENTIATED MIND-SET, DIFFERENTIATED FOCUS is key to success.

Above all, insist on having CONTINUITY, CONTINUITY, CONTINUITY in everything you do!

Chapter 9

Lesson Nine — Trust but Verify

Crafting the Creative Brief

"There is nothing more difficult to carry out, nor more doubtful of success, nor more dangerous to handle, than to institute a new order of things."

—Machiavelli

You're feeling "oh so cool." You've taken everything you know about your brand and infused it into one word or phrase—a powerful core value like Six Flags® did with *"Thrill"* (refer back to chapter eight for Six Flags positioning build). You've built a brand positioning platform that reflects a single-minded identity—from which everything you do will be planned, measured and evaluated. Now roll up your sleeves. The real work has just begun.

From a brand positioning platform evolves the CREATIVE BLUEPRINT or CREATIVE BRIEF. Marketers often have their own style or boilerplate for briefs, but the general content that is a MUST-HAVE in a well-designed creative brief is typically the same.

The Creative Brief should provide specific enough information to:

- guide ALL creative development, including look, logo, advertising, packaging, website, promotional, collateral materials, etc,
- quantify project objectives and outline the brand strategies,

- state clear target audience(s) with psychographic behavior segmentation,
- define any project barriers,
- highlight customer/consumer benefits,
- describe the brand promise—the brand's business proposition,
- define the tonality and/or visual style that appeals to the target audience

Why do a creative brief? In three words—*Focus, Consistency* and *Gut-Check.* Like it or not, most creative teams (especially outside agency support teams—i.e. advertising agencies, etc.) are a lot like dealing with the former Soviet Union back during the Cold War—you need to *"Trust but Verify!"*

CASE STUDY: *THE EXCELSIOR CORPORATION*

As an in-house business and marketing consultant for a decade old electronic payments credit card data processing company—call it *"The Excelsior Corporation"*—I started from the traditional planning position, the ground floor, while physically I was working at a desk high in the mix of towers in the company's headquarters located in midtown Manhattan. The first order of business was to design a brand positioning strategy using the brand positioning pyramid model (refer back to chapter eight), resulting in a strong *Core Value* or brand essence: *"Reassurance."* For consideration, exhibit 9-1 below illustrates what the brand positioning architecture for *"Excelsior Corporation"* could be that results in a *Core Value* described as *"Reassurance"* (note: *The Excelsior Corporation example is presented for learning purposes only and is not based on any specific brand's actual positioning strategy. With that said, given marketing expertise combined with some industry knowledge, this author would argue that the strategy presented is valid and worthy of consideration*).

Exhibit 9-1: *Excelsior Corporation* Brand Positioning Architecture

Exhibit 9-2 below defines a clear brand promise for *Excelsior* which might be crafted as a result of the brand architecture's positioning platform shown in Exhibit 9-1 above.

Exhibit 9-2: *Excelsior Corporation* Brand Promise

Excelsior Corporation
Brand Positioning Platform

Excelsior PROMISE

"Enriches the Automation and Security of the Merchant Account; never conceding on Real-Time Troubleshooting or Speed in Transaction Reconciliation."

Excelsior promised its customers a guarantee, that through its state-of-the-art technology, an understanding of their merchant customers' needs and challenges, and a unique customer service program, it would guarantee to be there for its merchant customers as well as its Independent Sales Offices, known as ISO's. Because the company prided itself on being the very best option for its merchant customers, it would guarantee that its products and staff of specialists would take away the worries and time-consuming chores associated with credit card processing, electronic check approvals, and related merchant time and bookkeeping costs of doing business.

Next, consider the brand's Creative Brief, beginning with the rationale for the company's Core Value—*'Reassurance.'*

Reassurance: *The act of boosting, restoring one's confidence. Acts as a Safeguard or Advocate for Encouragement, Protection and Security.*

and the Rationale ...

Excelsior Corporation is an advocate for the merchant. Excelsior promotes failsafe systems that allow merchants to bolster their transactions without hassle, without hesitancy and with an eye toward maximizing the average retail transaction size.

After writing this down in stone, I moved onto the next step.

The idea was simple. The status quo in the industry was for prototypical independent merchants, i.e., grocery retailers and restaurants, to move from one credit card processor to another depending on who was offering a lower processing fee, or who gave away new in-store credit card processing hardware terminals, or who happened to walk in their door the day they were fed up with problems with their current processor. *Excelsior* had such confidence in its technology, reliability and guaranteed quick resolution of merchant problems that it would promise its customers (current and potential customers) to be their last processor. In other words, the merchant would never have the need to switch credit card processors again.

Here's how it shapes-up as we begin to develop the full Creative Brief.

Brand Call-to-Action Platform

> *Excelsior Corporation* = *"Merchants for Life"*
> *"Work Smarter, Not Harder"*

What We Want to Say about the Brand

To merchants and Independent Sales Organizations—ISOs (those in the field who represent the processor to the merchant) ...

> *Excelsior* = *"People and Technology, Built around the way You Work"*

How We Want to Say It (brand communications tagline)

> Overall, *Excelsior Corporation* = ***"Reach Beyond"***

And specifically to a merchant's business,

> *Excelsior Corporation* is dedicated to *Reaching Far Beyond* the traditional ways of servicing their business—bookkeeping tools, cash advance programs, technology support, etc.

> *"Reach Beyond"* means ... going far beyond hardware/terminal giveaways and transaction fee gimmicks

> *"Reach Beyond"* means ... *innovation, automation, service* and *security* in every merchant transaction.

Working with the company's key sales management, we can draft a detailed set of behavior attributes as they relate to the *Excelsior Corporation's* primary target customers. Psychographics should be used to describe what their key motivations or key drivers are and demographics should be used for print (and potentially radio) media planning and placement.

From here, the Creative Brief can really begin to evolve and take full shape. Initially, it may contain outlines or headings with subheads and supporting statements. More and more detail will be added. For example, a section on *Advertising Copy Strategy* might start with the following guiding bullets, then be flushed out to provide for a more useful planning document.

Advertising Copy Strategy

- *Advertising Objectives*—quantifiable targets for the brand's health (i.e. unaided awareness, repeat purchase rates, etc.)
- *Current Brand Story*—what the company has traditionally, or is currently being, said about the brand—but isn't necessarily differentiating from competition
- *Desired Brand Story*—what we want to say about the brand—The *Brand Promise*
- *What We Say About the Brand*—The specific call-to-action
- *How We Speak About the Brand*—tonality of message
- *Execution Guidelines*—key considerations

Exhibit 9-3 below is a description of the key components of a proposed Creative Brief for *Excelsior Corporation*—demonstrating an example for a business-to-business entity. This is followed by Exhibit 9-4 which illustrates the Creative Brief for *Six Flags® Theme Parks*. The Six Flags brand is included here to demonstrate an example for a direct business-to-consumer entity. In the case of Six Flags, the creative brief is centered on the *THRILL* positioning (presented in chapter eight) and the umbrella call-to-action, *"You In, or You Out?"*

Exhibit 9-3: *Excelsior Corporation* Proposed Creative Brief

The Creative Brief

The Excelsior Corporation - Primary Target Customer(s)

Independent Retail Merchants & Level 2 ISO's*

- ✓ Self-Reliant/Self-Directing
- ✓ Technologically Savvy
- ✓ Take-Charge/Control-Oriented
- ✓ Relationship-Embracing
- ✓ Stability/Security-Seeking
- ✓ Ambitious/Achievers
- ✓ Realism Over Idealism
- ✓ Blend/Balance Work and Personal Life

* Note: Level 2 ISO's are *Independent Sales Offices* that represent middle-tier Agents driving 5-49 new data processing applications per month. This target achieves an average monthly sales volume of $100,000-$500,000.

Exhibit 9-3 continued

Excelsior Corporation - Advertising Copy Strategy

Advertising Objectives
✓ Drive Unaided Awareness & Trial among New Merchant Accounts. (Bricks 'n Mortar & On-Line)
✓ Build Image to recruit *Excelsior* direct-to-merchant Sales Agents new to industry, or from competitor brands.
✓ Build Brand Image/Drive Call-to-Action to recruit New Level 2 ISO Agents. (Customers)
✓ Reverse the Churn in Level 3 ISO's through business enhancing message. (Customers)
✓ Drive Continuity of message with existing *Royalty Partners (R.P.)* for retention/enhanced motivation & organic sales growth. (Customers)

Primary Target Audience - Recruitment/Non-R.P. Customers
✓ Retail Merchant Level for local market print and/or radio test – target independent grocers, restaurants, etc.
✓ Level 2 ISO's: Middle-tier offices doing 5-49 new applications per month or
$100K-$500K in processing per month

Secondary Target Audience – Re-inforcement/Existing R.P. Customers
✓ Royalty Partners/Level 1: Top-tier offices doing minimum 50 new applications
per month or $1.0 million+ in processing per month
✓ Level 3 ISO's: Bottom-tier offices doing < 5 new applications per month

Current Brand Story
✓ *Excelsior Corporation* is where ISO's want to be. *Excelsior* offers data processing products and services to Retail Merchants. *Excelsior* provides Merchants with the ability to accept all forms of payment, from credit and debit cards, to gift cards, to e-commerce, to government EBT cards.

Desired Brand Story
✓ *Excelsior Corporation* is your data processing brand of choice because it enriches the Automation and Security of the Merchant Account; never conceding on Real-Time Troubleshooting or Speed in Transaction Reconciliation.

What We Say About the Brand
✓ The *Excelsior Corporation's* tools, technology, training and systems acts as your reassurance, allowing you the merchant to *"Reach Beyond." Excelsior* is an advocate for the Merchant. *Excelsior* promotes failsafe systems that enables Merchants to bolster their transactions without hassle, without hesitancy and with an eye toward maximizing the average retail transaction size.

How We Speak About the Brand
✓ Real, dependable, innovator that is emotionally-charged, down-to-earth; Perhaps even a little self-deprecating.
✓ Believable/Recognizable/Memorable to the customer.
✓ Trustworthy enough to form habit-buying; drive word-of-mouth.

Executional Guidelines/Key Considerations
✓ Execute against the brand positioning?
✓ Print Medium with Long-term potential; extendibility to PR? Promotions?
✓ Distinct tagline/call to action (*'Reach Beyond'*)
✓ Drive new ISO business sales leads?

Exhibit 9-4: Six Flags Theme Parks Proposed Creative Brief

The Creative Brief

Example: Six Flags - Core Brand Target

Popularity Seekers (Loyal)

✓ Attracted to trendy, cutting edge, stylish brands (Nike, Apple, Calvin Klein, Aéropostale, MTV)
✓ Somewhat pretentious, insecure, self-conscious
✓ Skew younger, more Male
✓ Less price sensitive; buy on image; receptive to telemarketing
✓ Rebellious, self-indulgent, daring, irreverent

Relief Seekers (Vulnerable)

✓ Attracted to glamour brands (AMEX, Entertainment Weekly)
✓ Loyalty to escapist brands
✓ Buy on convenience, more than price; shop at niche, specialty stores
✓ Somewhat skeptical, yet opinionated
✓ More liberal, masculine
✓ Connect with Kobe, Beyoncé, A-Rod

Popularity and Relief Seekers are able to handle socializing with relative ease. They always seem to have a tribe of friends around. They seek products that make them more interesting and attractive to others. They seek escape to cope with difficulties in their lives.

SIX FLAGS® - Advertising Copy Strategy

Advertising Objectives
✓ Improve key value-for-money image ratings among "core-type" target consumers
✓ Drive first time trial/penetration rates among infrequent/receptive users
✓ Drive top-of-mind awareness and brand loyalty (repeat purchase rates) among repeat visitors

Target Audience - Core Consumers
✓ Psychographics: "Popularity & Relief Seekers"
✓ 1st Time Triers: 12 - 17 Year Olds
✓ Repeat Users: 18 – 24 Year Olds

Current Brand Story
✓ Six Flags is the convenient, close-to-home theme park option to Disney offering good value in rides and attractions and is fun for the whole family.

Desired Brand Story
✓ Six Flags is the theme park of choice because it heightens the thrill of any ride or attraction; never presenting a passive or deprivational environment. It combines cutting edge technology with Warner Bros. brands for the most exciting of interactive environments.

What We Say About the Brand
✓ Six Flags has escapists thrills that are right here, right now.

How We Speak About the Brand
✓ Thrilling, Youthful, Challenging, Irreverent

Executional Guidelines/Key Considerations
✓ Execute against the brand positioning?
✓ Clear linkage/understanding of Warner Bros. association?
✓ Long-term potential; extendibility to PR? Promotions?
✓ Distinct tagline/call to action (*'You in, or You Out?'*)
✓ Move business overnight?

Note the headings or components in Exhibits 9-3 and 9-4 are the same, it is in the specific details that the blueprint will always vary creative brief to creative brief.

In the final analysis, it is the Creative Brief, with as much actionable detail as possible, which will be translated into a new identity, a new message, a new campaign. In the case of *Excelsior Corporation*, a campaign, with the umbrella call-to-action, *"Reach Beyond"* could begin to create a new identity, a new promise that can be translated to advertising that directly targets merchant customers like grocery retailers, restaurants, furniture stores, clothiers, etc.

To illustrate, a campaign might begin in print ads with creative and copy points like the example *(created solely for learning purposes)* shown in Exhibit 9-5 below; expand to direct marketing materials; and ultimately lead to the platform for a tool kit for field sales and service staff—to better educate sales and support staff about *Excelsior* products and services, and how best sales can present those products and services to the merchant customer.

Exhibit 9-5: *Excelsior Corporation* print advertising — proposed example creative

REACH BEYOND 24/7/365

REACH for Excelsior 24/7/365. *We are a credit card processor that distinguishes itself by offering creativity and cutting-edge technology to maximize service. Featured in several business magazines' annual ranking as one of the fastest growing technology-based companies in the U.S., Excelsior® Corporation has people & technology, built around you.*

Reach far beyond with Titan, our merchant terminal interactive transaction software and accounting network tool. Titan promotes failsafe systems 24/7/365, thus enabling merchants to bolster their transactions without hassle, without hesitancy and with an eye toward maximizing their average transaction size. Titan automates monthly statements and bookkeeping—enabling merchants to work smarter, not harder in their quest to cultivate credit card using customers for life.

Excelsior means more revenues for you and greater growth for your business. To learn more, visit www.excelsiorprocessing.com.

Excelsior Corporation
Reach Beyond

Chapter 10

Lesson Ten—Framing the Cause in order to Do Battle

Introducing a New Approach to SWOT Analysis: Defining Must-Win-Battles

"Obstacles are Those Frightful Things You See When You Take Your Eyes off Your Goal."

—Henry Ford

The idea of using SWOT analysis for strategic planning that leads to a set of marketing initiatives is certainly not new. But while the concept is right, relying on the traditional SWOT definers—*Strengths, Weaknesses, Opportunities* and *Threats*—does not tell us enough to be truly meaningful, to be truly useful in the immediate term.

The problem with SWOT is that it attempts to provide us with an analysis of a brand's health without any direct relativity to the brand's key competition. Yes, after examining a brand through traditional SWOT we will have a nice neat list of opportunities (or potential initiatives). But it is likely to be a very long laundry list, without clear prioritization or the ability to capitalize on specific entries.

Consider the case of *Six Flags® Theme Parks*, a leading theme park company. Exhibit 10-1 below illustrates what results would likely develop as a marketing team waves through the traditional method to conducting SWOT—*Strengths, Weaknesses, Opportunities* and *Threats*.

Exhibit 10-1: Six Flags® SWOT Analysis Results — traditional method

SIX FLAGS® THEME PARKS
S. W. O. T. ANALYSIS

Strengths	Weaknesses
Geographic Coverage	Price / Value Perceptions
Interactive Environment	Lack of Consumer Focus
State-of-Art Ride Technology/Innovation	Quality Perceptions (Food, Safety, Staffing, etc.)
High Unaided Brand Awareness	Image vs. Disney
Season Pass / Repeat Purchase Rates	Seasonality
Warner Bros. (WB) Association	Speed / Rate of Capital Infusion
	Ticket Mix
Opportunities	**Threats**
Consumer Positioning that Differentiates	Weather Dependent
Seniors / Kids / Ethnic	Competitor Thrill Rides (Disney, Univ., Busch)
Value-added Promotions / Tie-ins	Non-Theme Park Entertainment (Local)
Drive Main Gate % of Business	Aging Park Infrastructure
Improve Advertising Effectiveness	
Brand Publicity Efforts (Consumer-Driven)	
Entertainment / Shows Development	
WB / Cartoon Network Imagery – Capital Infusion	
New Product Delivery Formats (i.e., Website)	

Notice how unmanageable the list of opportunities above can be for Six Flags—where is the focus—where is the clear way forward to driving the budget?

Consider a Better Way …

SWOT analysis can be considerably more meaningful, and in fact critical to strategic development and planning, if in the end it leads the manager to clearly define a brand's *"Must Win Battles"* (MWB's). My magic number is five. Present a clear set of up to five "Must Win Battles," and you can mobilize an entire organization, and its limited resources, in a very focused direction—and keep that organization on a disciplined path to business Utopia.

Michael Porter of the Harvard Business School said, *"The Essence of Strategy is that You Must Set Limits on What You're Trying to Accomplish. The Essence of Strategy is Choosing What Not to Do."* With a manageable set of core priorities, that every employee and every action can be measured against, well you can imagine the benefits. Everyone in the organization will live these Must-Win-Battles. Every action plan initiative will be measured against how well that initiative supports those MWB's. Even employee performance objectives will be tied to achieving the MWB's. With everyone on the same page, this is, bottom-line, meaningful analysis at its very best.

Remember, as is illustrated in Exhibit 10-2 below, the traditional approach to SWOT analysis fails to provide a clear focus in addressing brand issues against that of key competition. The new approach as shown in Exhibit 10-3 leads to a set of Must-Win-Battles that absolutely are targeted to address competition.

Exhibit 10-2: Traditional SWOT Analysis Approach

SWOT ANALYSIS

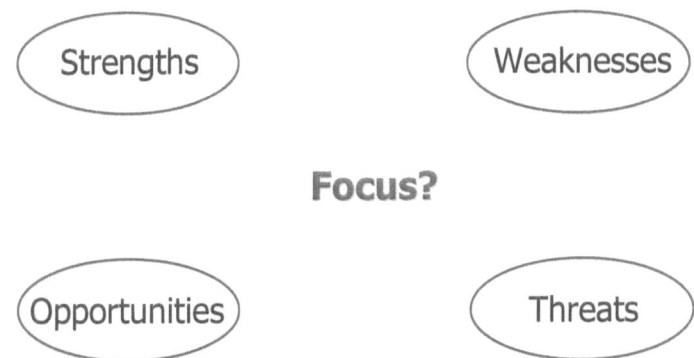

Instead consider the insights from Exhibit 10-3 below,

Exhibit 10-3: New SWOT Analysis Approach

SWOT ANALYSIS

Exhibit 10-4 below illustrates the building blocks associated with this new approach to conducting SWOT analysis. First, instead of SWOT's traditional analysis of defining a brand's Strengths, consider examining *Competitive Advantages*. Specifically, attempt to define the brand's *Competitive Advantages* in the areas of:

1. marketing/communications,

2. customer issues, and

3. operational structure

Exhibit 10-4 below illustrates the factors associated with each of the three categories above that will help shape and define your brand's Strengths in the context of *Competitive Advantages* relative to competition.

Exhibit 10-4: SWOT — What to Evaluate

SWOT – What To Evaluate?

Marketing and Communications

- ✓ Current marketing strategies and results
- ✓ Media coverage
- ✓ Available resources and/or budget
- ✓ Strategic alliances

Customer Issues

- ✓ Awareness of services
- ✓ Perceptions of services
- ✓ Satisfaction levels
- ✓ Ability to identify what services they want

Operational Structure

- ✓ Sophistication of programs/services
- ✓ Levels of expertise/staffing
- ✓ Partners roles and contributions
- ✓ Available services
- ✓ Customer service programs and procedures
- ✓ Internal communication structure

Likewise, instead of producing SWOT's traditional list of Weaknesses, consider the brand's *Vulnerabilities*, again, as they relate to the competition, and in each of the three category areas listed above in Exhibit 10-4. What's the difference between weaknesses and vulnerabilities? Lets assume your brand is Six Flags theme parks. What if your theme park has terrible food? Yes, this is a weakness. But is it also considered to be a vulnerability? People typically arrive at theme parks early and stay all day or into the evening. Visitors in long lines get bored and hungry. If the park has notoriously bad food (and probably high prices) people are more likely to bring their own food, or try to eat before they come and/or leave just before dinner. So the park's profits are vulnerable to the quality of its food, and especially if its closest competitor does not suffer that same vulnerability.

Now consider you are the marketing manager for concessions at a major league baseball park. The quality of available food is definitely a weakness. But is it a vulnerability? It's perceived as junk food—hot dogs that always give me indigestion, popcorn with much more salt than my doctor wants me to have. No juice for the kids, just sugary soda. But is food important at a ball game? Does it have any weight in the decision by a patron to go to a game or not or to spend money on this food once they're there? And isn't it actually part of the culture that would be missed if it changed? So food quality may be a weakness, but in this case, it may not be classified as being a vulnerability.

Next, traditional SWOT analysis evaluates Threats. Instead, look at a brand's *Eminent Risks*. Again, take the theme park scenario above as an example. A threat to the park is that it will rain Saturday and your potential guests will go to a movie theater instead. Obviously, there isn't much you can do about the rain, other than offer free rain ponchos.

But think harder about *Eminent Risks*. Is your closest competitor really the other major theme park three hours south? Consider that on any given Saturday or Sunday, or summer weekday, the closest competition is probably right in your own backyard. Instead of seeking out thrill rides today, your customers might decide to go to a movie theater or go to the shopping mall or to a games arcade. So an *Eminent Risk* is clearly that your park is closed for six months of the year, while your closest competitor, albeit indirect competition (i.e., the local movie theater and shopping mall) is marketing to your customers all year long.

This one example of *Eminent Risk* might lead to a place on your very short list of Must-Win-Battles—to reach your target audience with park excitement year round. Perhaps you launch a park-themed, web-based initiative that presents Teens with a series of games or contests marketed to them throughout the year. Now you have continued the excitement of your brand, your theme park, even when you're not open. Or, perhaps your park creates a year-round co-branding promotion with a product or entertainment service that markets to your customers throughout the year. Maybe a video game is developed that is clearly identified as played in your park. Maybe it's given away as a special promotion with every 10 video rentals through a retailer like *Blockbuster*®, or with every 10 subs at *Subway*® Sub Shops. You get the idea.

Bringing it all together, once you have identified your brand's *Competitive Advantages, Vulnerabilities* and *Eminent Risks*, versus competition, these factors or components should easily lead you to a set of *Must-Win-Battles*. In other words, Must-Win-Battles evolve from the combination of *Competitive Advantages, Vulnerabilities* and *Eminent Risks* and are not independent of them. That bears repeating ... MWB's evolve from the combination of *Competitive Advantages, Vulnerabilities* and *Eminent Risks* and are not independent of them.

Exhibit 10-5 below illustrates the results of the Six Flags example under the new SWOT approach. Think about how the much more focused set of Must-Win-Battles might enable Six Flags to more effectively rally its organization against a common strategic thrust.

Exhibit 10-5: Six Flags results under new SWOT approach

SIX FLAGS® THEME PARKS
S. W. O. T. ANALYSIS

Competitive Advantages	Vulnerabilities
Geographic Coverage	Speed / Rate of Capital Infusion (new Rides)
Interactive Environment	Quality Perceptions (Food, Safety, Staffing, etc.)
Warner Bros. (WB) Association	Seasonality
Must Win Battles	**Eminent Risks**
Consumer Positioning that Differentiates	Weather Dependent
Improve Advertising Effectiveness	Non-Theme Park Entertainment (Local)
Value-added Promotion in place of discounts	
Drive Main Gate % of Business	
WB / Cartoon Network Imagery – Capital Infusion	

This new approach to SWOT analysis never underestimates the importance of relativity to competition. Think about it. If the brand manager has identified that the brand's strongest strength, or weakest weakness, is the same as that of his/her nearest competitor, that brand manager may decide that the situation presents a marketing opportunity, or conversely, that because they negate each other, it is not advantageous to leverage this particular strength or address this particular weakness at this time. As this illustrates, your strategies, your Must-Win-Battles, are likely to be very different than if you merely identified your own brand's strengths and weaknesses, without regard to their relativity to competition. It may seem elementary, but the traditional components of SWOT analysis fall short in this critical area of differentiation and relativity.

Why is SWOT analysis such an important tool for successful marketing strategy development? In one word: *Manageable.* It leads us to a manageable number of key initiatives to fund. Obviously we need strategies. We go through this process to generate a focused set of Must-Win-Battles, which in essence become strategic brand thrusts, and ultimately key action initiatives that require budget funding. How else would you suggest we arrive at brand strategies? Should we, as many companies do, repeat last year's strategies, from last year's brand plan?

Marketing Czar 101: using last year's strategies appears to others that you didn't get last year's job done. After all, as we will illustrate further in chapter twelve, those strategies you craft should be designed to address a set of brand key issues and challenges. If successful, then the next year's plan would not be a simple repeat of the past year's plan. Make sense?

I suggest you stop and take your own brand through the SWOT exercise using the new evaluation tools outlined above in Exhibit 10-4. Address each topic or issue both for your own brand and if possible that of your brand's nearest competitor(s). See the difference in your SWOT results and see the clear way forward in rallying the entire organization against a renewed strategic focus inherent in your company's Must-Win-Battles?

Once you have gone through this systematic exercise, and you have created a Must-Win-Battles set of strategic initiatives, check them against the prototypical set of MWB's in Exhibit 10-6 below from crafting SWOT the new way. Use this as a starting point, a bench mark when developing your own brand's set of MWB's. Notice the difference? Chances are that most, if not all, of your Must Win Battles will fall within the set of categories outlined in Exhibit 10-6.

Exhibit 10-6: Prototypical Must-Win-Battles

Prototypical **Must Win Marketing Battles**

✓ Reduce/eliminate margin-eroding programs (i.e. price promotions)

✓ Partner with Customers (i.e. Retailers) to Drive Profitable Growth

✓ Generate Fuel for Growth (i.e. cut costs, build partnerships/alliances)

✓ Broaden Distribution/Enhance Visibility (i.e. merchandize out-of-aisle)

✓ Own Emerging Specialty/Niche Markets (i.e. Seniors, Teens, Ethnic)

Now that you have identified your focused set of priorities, never underestimate their power. Make it your own Must-Win-Battle to integrate them into every facet of your company or organization. Consider it an internal communications highest priority to educate everyone from chief executive to managers to subordinates to supervisors and trainers to know by heart and to truly live by the company's Must-Win-Battles—to buy into the importance of measuring every action plan in every functional area against them.

Before long, you will begin to see the results of an integrated corporate strategy across the company, and in the eyes of your own bosses, you will appear to have won a significant battle of your own.

Chapter 11

Lesson Eleven — It's Better to Give Birth to a New Baby then to try and Resuscitate a Dead Man

Innovating with the New Product Development Growth Strategy Model

"Innovation is THE central issue in economic prosperity."

—Michael Porter, Harvard Business School

So, you've decided to plan for "a baby." The ones we're talking about here might take nine months to develop, but they aren't usually warm, wet or wrapped in either pink or blue.

What you're planning for here is the launch of a new product. But why not just try to revitalize the tired brand you currently have? *"Because it's better to give birth to a new baby then it is to try and resuscitate a dead man."* Chances are that when you and your brand team utilized the *Brand Activation Matrix* (refer back to chapter seven), new product development (NPD) was born or confirmed as a critical key initiative. Most likely, NPD opportunities appear in the upper left quadrant with *"Hide and Seek"* brands, where a brand has low relative market share, yet there is high relative brand equity. But clearly there are new product development opportunities elsewhere within the *Brand Activation Matrix* strategy model like the case for *"Attention Getter"* brands to expand its product uses or usage occasions.

And now you are faced with the critical choice of what strategies to choose for developing your new baby. The matrix tool illustrated in Exhibit 11-2 below is useful in choosing the right new product growth strategy, given the economics of the market opportunities and the motivations of your customers (existing and potential).

The purpose of the exercise is to develop *"Hot Spots."* Personally, I like to lock a brand team in a room with me, a flip chart and a marker. *"Tell me about our current customers,"* I'd say. Then we proceed to make a long list of the target customers' attributes. Next, we do the same for what we describe as our *"potential customers."* This simple exercise will help identify our marketing *Hot Spots*, which we will then evaluate within the New Product Development (NPD) Growth Strategy Matrix Model tool shown below, near the end of this chapter, in Exhibit 11-2.

So, as general manager for *Ragu® Pasta Sauce* a few years back, that same flip chart work told us that a most important customer of the brand were *women on the go*. They needed convenience in a food product. They wanted quick foods for a family meal and instant, yet healthy, snack foods they could serve from products they always had in the cupboard. On the chart next to *"on-the-go-moms,"* we identified two critical opportunity *Hot Spots*: (1) snacks alternative and (2) new product meal solutions packaged as all-in-one meals. From these two *Hot Spots,* several new product initiatives were born, fully-developed, beta tested and marketed for launch.

At *Smirnoff®*, back in the mid-1990's, the status quo was its classic 80 proof vodka, the market leader in the traditional red label. When we listed our customers and potential customers on a flip chart, three standout *Hot Spots* emerged. First, younger drinkers wanted flavors in *"so cool"* packaging. Second, the traditional Smirnoff drinker was aging. They would be more likely to buy a larger bottle to keep on-hand if they could carry it home in lighter plastic packaging. Third, the *on-the-go* potential customer chose beer because of its portability. The *"ready-to-drink"* (RTD) market was hot, as was the development, marketing and launch of several Smirnoff RTD initiatives, which led to today's success with *Smirnoff Ice®*.

Exhibit 11-1 below is the New Product Development Growth Strategy Model for Smirnoff® Vodka. Note how we have identified opportunities across several segments.

Exhibit 11-1: Smirnoff® NPD Growth Strategy

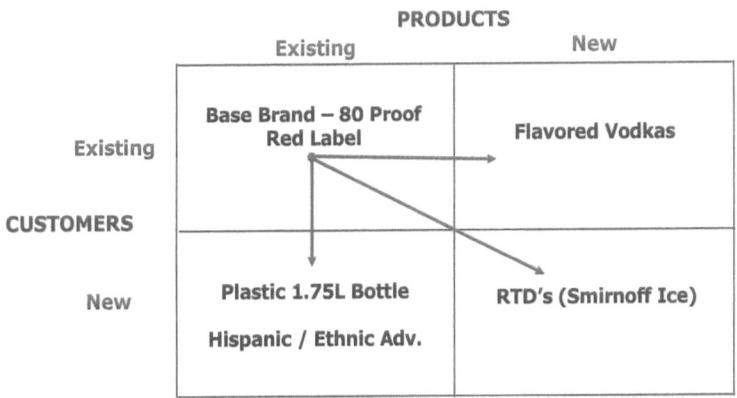

Smirnoff ®
NPD Growth Strategy

PRODUCTS

First look at what is *Status Quo* position of your brand. This is a look at what existing products you offer to your existing customers. The easiest strategy for growth from here is a *Market Penetration* strategy—to further penetrate the market with your existing products. So in the lower left quadrant you develop ideas with your existing products that attract new prospective customers. Who are these untapped customers? Are there geographic regions where your distribution is weak? Are there age groups, economic or ethnic/cultural groups you aren't reaching? Now, what will you have to do to your existing product to market to one or more of these new customers, i.e., unique packaging, ethnic marketing (i.e. Hispanic), etc.

The following Matrix illustrates the point.

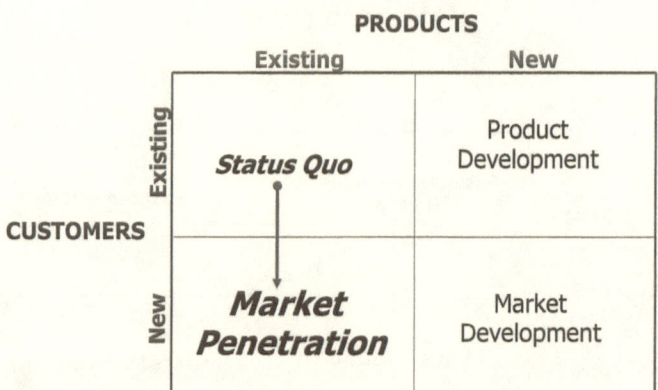

New Product Development
Growth Strategy Matrix

The most common brand growth strategy is brand extension—you present a new product to your existing customers. These ideas sit in the upper right quadrant. The strategic challenge here is one of *Product Development*. This can be reviewed in the matrix below.

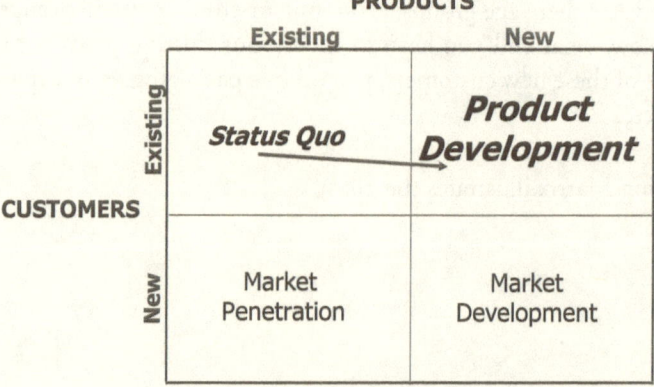

New Product Development
Growth Strategy Matrix

Last, and most difficult, is the strategic challenge of *Market Development*, when you set out to present a new product to a new customer. But if you sit where *Mercedes Benz®* sat, where your relative brand equity is so high that potential customers would be thrilled (or at least pleased) to have access to your brand, you may be in a position to go for the challenge, as Mercedes Benz did with the development of its C-Class. Clearly it is the most expensive and time-consuming strategy for new product development, yet with perhaps the greatest long-term potential—carrying the greatest ROI.

See the matrix below for illustration of a *Market Development* growth strategy.

New Product Development Growth Strategy Matrix

PRODUCTS

	Existing	New
CUSTOMERS Existing	*Status Quo*	Product Development
New	Market Penetration	*Market Development*

Finally, Exhibit 11-2 below illustrates the NPD Growth Strategy Matrix Model in full form.

Exhibit 11-2: The New Product Development Growth Strategy Matrix Model

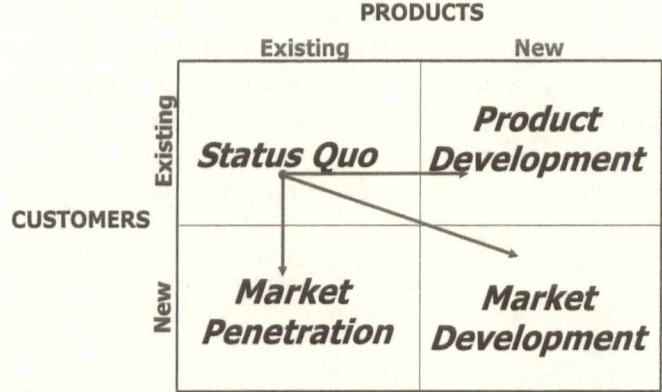

What is critical to remember here is that whichever growth strategy path or paths you take to expand your brand's opportunities, not everything will work—and that is okay. With failure comes learning and with learning comes better odds for success the next go around. Case in point—Smirnoff's venture into the RTD category did not begin and end with the success of Smirnoff Ice. Smirnoff had tried and experienced at least two other false starts (Smirnoff Singles and Smirnoff Mule) in the ready-to-drink segment before fielding a winner with Smirnoff Ice.

So, in NPD be bold, be bold—but in NPD be smart, be smart and learn from failures and have the wisdom to ride fewer winners to experience greater ROI.

Chapter 12

Lesson Twelve—Think Global, Plan Regional, but Act Local
Utilizing the Marketing Plan Template

"If you have built castles in the air, your work need not be lost; that is where they should be. Now put foundations under them."

—Henry David Thoreau

It may seem elementary at this point to talk about the importance of developing a strategic marketing plan. But sometimes the most obvious is worth repeating. The truth is that a well conceived strategic plan is priceless—worth all of the time and effort involved in the exercises and outcomes that led up to the finished product.

A strategic marketing plan, if nothing else, enables the organization to:

- provide clear direction
- avoid internal duplication of efforts
- objectively identify brand strengths and weaknesses
- target communication efforts
- provide a strong evaluation component
- prioritize key marketing mix elements, initiatives and related budgets

The marketing plan template provided here is the one I like to use. It's simple, straightforward, yet comprehensive. Think of it as a set of building blocks, with each component, top to bottom, left to right, building on the articulation of the building blocks that preceded it.

While every building block here plays an important role, we'll concentrate on the second block—*Lessons Learned* and *Key Issues & Challenges*. The reason is quite simple. This is the bread and butter of the plan. If you don't identify and quantify key issues, you can't move forward to strategies or action plan initiatives in support of those strategies.

Said differently, any marketing plan's strategies should be designed to address a key issue & challenge. That way, you know if your strategies are working because you can measure its impact by whether it successfully addressed a key brand issue or merely a symptom of that issue.

Below in Exhibit 12-1, you can review the critical components or building block categories that make up a comprehensive marketing plan. This "template" includes not only a comprehensive financial review of the product/service category you compete in, but it also includes a thorough analysis of your key competitors—both direct and indirect, as well as an opportunity to list out what information gaps exists—i.e. own-brand and cross-price elasticity, customer/consumer NEED States, market by market performance measurements like brand and category development indices, etc.

The *Lessons Learned* and *Key Issues & Challenges* component to the annual marketing plan springboards from the first building block—the comprehensive *Competitive Analysis*. The *Lessons Learned* and *Key Issues & Challenges* building block is highlighted below because it is especially important as this particular building block provides the marketing team with a common set of problem areas that key initiatives need to be designed—and funded—to formidably address.

Also, the *Competitive Analysis* building block leads the marketing team to a better strategic result when conducting SWOT analysis for crafting *Must-Win-Battles* per the new approach as described earlier back in chapter ten.

Exhibit 12-1: The Marketing Plan Template

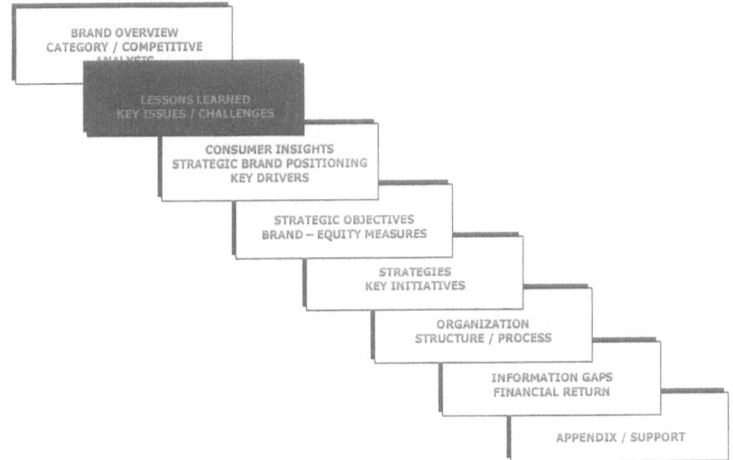

MARKETING PLAN TEMPLATE

BRAND OVERVIEW
CATEGORY / COMPETITIVE
ANALYSIS

LESSONS LEARNED
KEY ISSUES / CHALLENGES

CONSUMER INSIGHTS
STRATEGIC BRAND POSITIONING
KEY DRIVERS

STRATEGIC OBJECTIVES
BRAND – EQUITY MEASURES

STRATEGIES
KEY INITIATIVES

ORGANIZATION
STRUCTURE / PROCESS

INFORMATION GAPS
FINANCIAL RETURN

APPENDIX / SUPPORT

Lessons Learned

This exercise in marketing planning called *Lessons Learned* is simply a guide to keeping a historical discussion focused. The task is to outline the lessons the past year, or recent history, have taught the brand team. Exhibit 12-2 below illustrates several key areas to address to help keep you on track.

Exhibit 12-2: Annual Plan Lessons Learned

Lessons Learned

Suggested Key Areas to Address:

✓ Pricing / price discounting

✓ Consumer insights ➔ What works? What doesn't work?

✓ Why haven't previous triers returned?

✓ Competitive mix ➔ Direct Brand vs. In-Direct Competition

Key Issues & Challenges

After beating the above *Lessons Learned* to a pulp, you are ready to move on. Addressing the brand's key issues and challenges is essentially the single most influential task in the creation of a comprehensive strategic marketing plan. The purpose is to address each of the areas highlighted below in Exhibit 12-3, with the outcome being a list of key issues, each with a quantified impact, and an associated implication to the fiscal year plan. In other words, if I'm the chief marketing officer in the room, and you want to present a key issue, don't waste my time if you can't quantify it. I don't want to hear that we're missing an opportunity that our closest competitor has captured if you can't quantify for the company how much it's costing our business on the bottom line, and/or how much the company can expect to gain (enhanced revenues, incremental profit contribution) from jumping into this opportunity ourselves.

Exhibit 12-3: Annual Plan Key Issues & Challenges

Key Issues and Challenges

KEY ISSUES	QUANTIFIED IMPACT	IMPLICATIONS TO FISCAL YEAR PLAN

Suggested Key Areas To Address:

- ✓ Brand positioning within overall company/portfolio strategic plan
- ✓ Price discounting - How to dial back?
- ✓ Product mix shift to Core business - How to drive more Base Brand volume?
- ✓ Underdeveloped audiences - Seniors / Kids / Ethnic / Etc.

Here's the reward. Put your time into the exercise above. Produce a meaningful, well researched, well thought out list of quantifiable key issues and challenges. Now you will move on to articulate your brand's strategies and from this you will develop the key initiatives that require funding. But now you have a built-in sounding board—a measurement tool against which you can second-guess yourself to be sure your identified initiatives are on target.

As you develop key initiatives, you can debate how they do (or do not) relate to your key issues and challenges. If any do not relate, move on down the line and debate the next group of initiatives your team suggests for funding. You've just saved yourself at least several months of planning, and maybe even implementing, an initiative that wasn't worth your team's management time or your brand's budget expense.

Exhibit 12-4 below illustrates the critical components or *"directional development"* for each planning block, to help you create a better, more meaningful strategic marketing plan. Be assured, the time you spend on a new plan will be well worth it when next year you realize how much more focused your initiatives were this past year. And when your performance bonus and possible promotion are directly linked to the greater success of your extraordinarily focused brand team and measurable results, you're certain to look back in awe of all of that planning time, and conveniently forget the dread that overshadowed its onset.

Exhibit 12-4: Annual Marketing Plan — Directional Development

Marketing Plan Template
Directional Development

1. **Brand Overview / Category / Competitive Analysis**
   - Historical volumes and average transaction per cap trends
   - Plan year volume and average transaction per cap forecasts with rationale
   - Competitive analysis including anticipated strategic moves / emphasis

2. **Lessons Learned / Key Issues / Challenges**
   - At minimum, include areas to address as designated in Exhibits 12-2 and 12-3
   - Quantify impact of local issues
   - Assess implications to Plan

3. **Consumer Insights / Strategic Brand Positioning / Key Drivers**
   - Benchmark OWN-BRAND against key competitors - focus on key drivers of business

4. **Strategic Objectives / Brand-Equity Measures**
   - At minimum, include areas to address as (or like those) designated in Exhibit 12-5
   - Forecast volumes, resource support, financial return by type of customer
   - Set stretchable targets for key brand health measures and identify key initiative(s) to drive performance

5. **Strategies / Key Initiatives**
   - For strategies, at minimum, include areas to address as designated in Exhibit 12-6
   - For key initiatives, pay particular attention to Price Discount program justification.
   - Develop local consumer promotion/value-added calendar as overlay to proposed national promotion/national value-added calendar
   - Develop P&L's in support of local sponsorship programs

6. **Organization Structure / Process**
   - Articulate how you would recommend achieving functional excellence in each area- Brand Development, Revenue Development, Marketing Analysis, Consumer Orientation

7. **Information Gaps / Financial Return**
   - Identify key information gaps as they pertain to driving against the overall Corporate Strategy as illustrated in Exhibit 12-7 prototypical examples

8. **Appendix / Support**
   - Detailed back-up in support of planned initiatives

Exhibit 12-5: Annual Plan Strategic Objectives

Strategic Objectives / Financial Return

Suggested Key Areas to Address:

✓ Solidify *"Core-Type"* user Image Attribute ratings / repeat user rates
✓ Drive higher average transaction sizes with *"Core-Type"* users
✓ Grow opportunistic *"Infrequent Triers"* that are receptive
✓ Improve local promotional effectiveness

	Full Retail	Seasonal	Group Sales	Promotional	Multi-Pak Purch.	Other?
Volume						
AMP Support ($)						
Price Per Unit						
Revenue Per Purch.						
EBITDA Per Unit						

Exhibit 12-6: Annual Plan Brand Strategies

Brand Strategies

Suggested Key Areas to Address:

✓ Value-for-Money position

✓ Building image / top of mind awareness

✓ Average transaction size

✓ Non-discounted volume percent of business

✓ Value-added promotion/special events

✓ Recruiting new users / increasing repeat rates

Exhibit 12-7: Annual Plan Information Gaps — Prototypical Examples

Information Gaps

- ✓ Price elasticity measures
    - ✓ **Own-brand and cross-price elasticities by market**

- ✓ Consumer need states
    - ✓ **Segmentation analysis**
    - ✓ **Decision-process for category out-of-pocket dollar allocation**

- ✓ Brand Development Indices/Category Development Indices - BDI's/CDI's (or similar measures)

- ✓ Brand positioning / product mix breakdown
    - ✓ **Core offering vs. line-extensions against targeted consumer NEEDS / segments**

- ✓ Marketability of special themed events

- ✓ Value-for-money need states
    - ✓ **Own-brand discounting vs. competition**

Keep this mind, the annual marketing plan is intended to be a fluid document. It is intended to provide for flexibility as market conditions change. Good plans are designed to improve both marketing and organizational effectiveness—always with the intention of building brand equity.

Effective brand planning enables the marketing team to envision a new future—one where the company is:

- ✓ *Capturing consumer needs/behavior*, not simply driving volume at any cost.

- ✓ Developing marketing plans that are not simply an extension of past trends; need to break out of this mold and *re-invent the business.*

- ✓ Providing marketing *leadership from corporate*; not dictating from top.

- ✓ Championing bigger ideas that are fully integrated—advertising, promotion, PR and focused against a brand-equity building strategy; *status quo is not an option.*

- ✓ Achieving fiscal year plan results which drives momentum; *momentum builds motivation; motivation breeds success.*

A Final Word

Turn the Tigers Loose

Building Coalitions — Leadership from the Marketing Ranks

"In the long history of humankind (and animalkind, too) those who learned to collaborate and improvise most effectively have prevailed."

—Charles Darwin

It is my belief that marketing needs *RADICALS, REBELS* and *REVOLUTIONARIES*. People who *"HOWL AT THE MOON."* After all, high performance marketing teams are not born. They are raised from a philosophy—from a set of core beliefs that include:

- *Leadership*—*having the courage of one's convictions so that great ideas don't get watered down in implementation. Also, gaining buy-in early from above saves you aggravation in times when it is too late to change course.*

- *Change Agenda*—*last year's plan does not guarantee this year's success and more of the same will no longer catch competition off guard.*

- *Bias Toward Action*—*yes it is better to be first to market than it is to be better than competition.*

- *Management by Wandering Around (MBWA)*—*be visible to your team, especially those in the lower ranks, in order to gain their confidence and enable them to freely express ideas.*

- *Turn The Tigers Loose*—*allowing subordinates the opportunity to fail; the opportunity to circumvent current processes, and rewarding, not stifling, ideas that challenge the current ways of doing business.*

- ***Ideas Count; Process Sucks***—*internal process does not drive top-line sales; breakthrough thinking does!*

- ***Integration, Not Separation***—*brand planning must include representation from finance, sales, R&D and manufacturing in order to gain collective buy-in.*

- ***Controlled Chaos***—*don't let fighting today's fires get in the way of staying focused on working the big picture—always keep the big win in sight.*

- ***Mutual Respect***—*no ideas are bad ideas because your own ideas can't be bad, right?*

- ***Zero Tolerance***—*once the agenda is set and the plan-of-attack is agreed everyone must execute—no second guessing!*

- ***Working Hard or Working Smart?***—*trying to get noticed by arriving at the office early and leaving late does not guarantee success—breakthrough strategies and great ideas guarantee success!*

John Wooden the former UCLA Basketball Coach who holds a Record 10 National Championships is credited with saying, *"success is a function of skill, confidence and enthusiasm, and for any team to be successful all three—skill, confidence and enthusiasm—must be present."* Coach Wooden was correct then and he is correct now. No team, in sports or in business, can be successful if its key players are not skilled to compete, lack the confidence to express their ideas or haven't got the enthusiasm to see the plan through to fruition. What does this mean to the marketing leader? Simply that as brand marketing leaders we must instill into the organization a set of behavior attributes that ensure success. Five critical attributes for success come to mind:

First, ***Challenging the Process***

- ✓ Experimenting/Taking Calculated Risks—new ideas will inspire others and catch competition off guard.
- ✓ Searching for New Opportunities—always think out-of-the-box.

Next, ***Inspiring a Shared Vision***

- ✓ Building Coalitions by Enlisting Finance, Supply Chain, Manufacturing and R&D in the recommendation process—that way they are on the hook to deliver the goods, just as you are.
- ✓ Envisioning the Future with Passion—show the organization what tomorrow will look like while acting on today.

Third, **Enabling Others to Act**

✓ Strengthening Others by Delegating Authority—trust others to get the job done and nine out of ten times they will get the job done.

✓ Fostering Collaboration—cross-fertilize your team with that of other departments and/or outside agencies such that everyone is marching to the same tune, playing from the same song sheet.

Fourth, **Modeling the Way**

✓ Setting an Example by Listening, Listening, Listening—if you expect to be Heard, Heard, Heard.

✓ Planning Small Wins for Confidence Building—early fiscal year wins keeps everyone excited, focused and away from job-searching.

Fifth, **Encouraging the Heart**

✓ Publicly Recognizing Contributions—people want to know that their time with the organization is well spent; that they are doing a good job.

✓ Celebrating Milestones/Accomplishments—people want to know that what they are doing is actually important and that their efforts are contributing to the achievement of bigger goals.

There are several ways to accomplish all the above but one of my favorites is to conduct an exercise called *GITS*—"get into the skin of someone else." Here, if the manager is trying to get buy-in from others in the organization, it is likely helpful for the manager to think like the other person. Thus *GITS*—"get into the skin of someone else" means that the manager is trying to put himself or herself in the place of others—perhaps the company CEO or CFO or CMO or sales executive or finance director. Put yourself in the place of anyone in the organization that is a key influencer or decision maker.

What the manager should do is ask themselves, what does this person value? What does this person, say the company CFO, value professionally and what does this person value personally? Why do this? The idea is to try and understand the person better such that you can influence that person more effectively because you are in better tune with how they think and why they think a certain way. GITS—"get into the skin of someone else" so that you "become that person," sharing their values and understanding their motivations. That way, you gain the upper hand in the back and forth game of influencing the thinking and behavior of others.

FINAL THOUGHTS ON LEADERSHIP

Effective Leadership has been studied in the past and researched to what seems like no end. The facts on this subject are real—*"If You Don't Create Change, Change Will Create You."*

And when it comes to managing people, recall again the words of Ronald Reagan who said, *"Facts are Stubborn Things."* And the facts are—People don't want to be managed—They want to be Led! Whoever heard of a World Manager? World Leader, Yes! If you want to manage somebody, manage yourself. Do that and you will be ready to start Leading Others! The most effective managers Lead—They don't manage. Remember this—*"The carrot always wins over the stick—Just ask your Horse!"*

READY TO BE A BRAND CZAR?

My hope is that this work has better enabled you to become a more successful brand marketer. Are you now ready to be a Brand Czar? If you think you are now ready to be a true Brand Czar, then you must be ready and able to turn the tiger inside of you loose and live by and work toward the following edict:

> *"Marketing is Not a Spectator Sport. It is not administrative in its core value. It is about ideas, and it is about having the courage to think, look and act different from competition."*

Build Your Own Brand Plan!

Order a Complete CD-R of the Marketing Plan Template

MARKETING PLAN TEMPLATE

- BRAND OVERVIEW
  CATEGORY / COMPETITIVE ANALYSIS
- LESSONS LEARNED
  KEY ISSUES / CHALLENGES
- CONSUMER INSIGHTS
  STRATEGIC BRAND POSITIONING
  KEY DRIVERS
- STRATEGIC OBJECTIVES
  BRAND – EQUITY MEASURES
- STRATEGIES
  KEY INITIATIVES
- ORGANIZATION
  STRUCTURE / PROCESS
- INFORMATION GAPS
  FINANCIAL RETURN
- APPENDIX / SUPPORT

Includes the complete template for making use of all the relevant planning models presented through-out this book and highlighted in Chapter 12.

The brand planning template combines the ease of using PowerPoint slides with an interactive component in EXCEL. The EXCEL template can be altered/edited to accommodate your unique internal company needs and industry nuances.

We guarantee you will find this Template to be a valuable brand planning tool for your company and/or your client company brands!

To receive your CD-R of the Marketing Template for Annual Brand Planning, Simply tear-out this page and fill-out the information below and mail your order to the Savino Global Group address shown along with a **check or money order in ($) U.S. dollars made payable to *Savino Global Group, LLC.* Each CD-R planning template costs just $19.95 (price includes all shipping & handling).**

Your First Name: _____

Your Last Name: _____

Company Name: _____

Your Mailing Address: _____

City/State/Zip Code: _____

Total # of CD-R's Ordered: _____   Total Amount Due $ _____

Mail check and form to: Savino Global Group, LLC.
1040 Avenue of the Americas
24ᵗʰ Floor
New York, New York 10018

Please allow 4-6 weeks for delivery. This offer is subject to change without notice.

The goal of Savino Global Group is to meet and exceed your expectations by delivering the highest quality service and products.

Your complete satisfaction is guaranteed.

978-0-595-48453-9
0-595-48453-0

www.ingramcontent.com/pod-product-compliance
Lightning Source LLC
Chambersburg PA
CBHW030840180526
45163CB00004B/1402